THE TRANSFORMATIONAL
COLLEGE
EXPERIENCE

How to Make the Most of It

DANTE DIBATTISTA

ISBN: 979-8-9879618-0-3 (Print)
ISBN: 979-8-9879618-2-7 (Ebook)

Cover Design: VeryMuchSo.Agency

This book is dedicated to three beautiful souls,
whose memories I carry with me:

Ray Bailey
John Zackowski
Domenica Meloni

I lost all three of them during my college journey. All three of their stories
are woven into the fabric of the bindings that keep these pages together.
There would be no *me* without *them;* there would be no story. I hope that,
by sharing my perspective in the only way I know how, I can carve their
memories into the walls of time, so their legacies may outlast me.

To you, reader, I ask you to pause to check on those you love. I don't care if
that means putting this book down right this moment. The most important
lessons are taught through the love of others, especially those closest to you.

Cherish the stories they tell, even if they tell the same story over and over
again. No one will tell it quite like they do. Listen closely when they speak,
not just to their voice but to their body language and their energy. Sometimes
the loudest cries for help are communicated in silence.

**A percentage of every book sale will be donated to the American
Foundation for Suicide Prevention, in honor of Ray.**

**A percentage of every book sale will be donated to the American Diabetes
Association, in honor of John.**

**A percentage of every book sale will be donated to the Sons of Italy
Foundation, in honor of my grandmother, Domenica.**

Thank you for your contribution.

Contents

Introduction

Whether you're currently attending college or you're preparing for your freshman year, you probably already know that the college experience is a time of *transition* as you shift from high school adolescence to the freedoms and responsibilities of adulthood. But what if your college experience could be more than just a time of transition? What if these years could be an opportunity for *transformation*—a chance for you to create a solid foundation for creating your best life, now and into your future?

That is exactly what I hope to help you achieve with this book. I have made it my personal mission to help you create a life filled with happiness and success, *as you choose to define those terms*. Happiness and success look different for everyone, and college is a unique opportunity to explore the possibilities of who you are and build the foundation for your dreams to stand on. For most people, college marks the beginning of living a life on their own, one they will continue for decades thereafter. The mindset shifts, organizational skills, good habits, and personal connections you'll establish during this period will have profound impacts on your independent adult life.

If you are just beginning your journey, I want to impart some wisdom I've gained from my own painful experience of failing school—and generally failing at life—through my evolution to becoming a dean's list student and campuswide leader, and then becoming an unlikely success story with a thriving leadership consulting company, worldwide speaking engagements, and one of the top podcasts globally.

If you are already attending college, you may be struggling like I did, and as you read this book, you will find that you are not alone. I hope this book gives you the confidence to get back up and pursue your self-actualization—to become the most that you can be—with ferocity. I'll provide all of the strategies you need to make the most of your efforts, and I'll be here to support you along the way.

When I was around your age, I felt imprisoned by my own immaturity, and I thought I was surrounded by people who had it all figured out. I was wrong—twice: first, I was *not* trapped; and second, I came to find that most of the people around me only *appeared* to have it all figured out. Anyone who is recently out of high school and claims to have their life figured out is, in my opinion, thousands of miles farther away from the truth than the person who admits they have no idea what they are doing. This book will show you why almost every single college student (yes, even the best and the brightest) approaches school with the wrong mindset and fails to squeeze all of the juice out of the experience. I'll teach you how to avoid following their lead so that, one day, they will be following yours.

The Bait and Switch of the College Experience

A college education is one of the most expensive purchases you will ever make in your life, second only to buying a house. Just imagine: you've spent years saving up for a house, and then you spend several more months researching houses, seeing where you can get the most bang for your buck, and creating a list of everything you need or want from a house. After months of searching, you think you've found the one. You do a walk-through, and everything looks great. You put in the offer, it gets accepted, and you are so excited. You go through the whole process of buying the house (which is extremely stressful, by the way). Finally, this house that checked all of the boxes is finally yours. Suddenly, you get ready to move in and you find yourself moving into a completely different house. It no longer checks any of your boxes, but there's nothing you can do about it—the sale is final.

That is what is happening with today's college experience. Students are being sold an experience that isn't real. Over the years, college has been misbranded and sold as something it was never meant to be in the first place.

We were told that college is the key to getting a good job, yet students are graduating and are unable to get a job in their field. And if they are lucky enough to find a job related to their major, they aren't making enough money to pay back their loans—and sometimes they are worse off than they would have been if they had graduated high school and worked a minimum-wage job for those four (or five) years.

This book will break down many of the misconceptions that have created this problem, and it will give you real solutions to ensure you don't end up in that same position after graduation.

You may be asking yourself, *what makes this guy so sure he is the right person to tell this story, to write this book?* Well, I specialize in helping business and educational leaders build transformational cultures in their offices and classrooms. And I've become a thought leader in transformational leadership by starting with working on myself. I was on the road to self-destruction, and the results that have followed my transformational experience have been nothing short of spectacular.

As an avid reader, I would never tell you a story that's unworthy of reading. Even as I write this, I almost can't believe I've made it to this point. To give you an idea of where I started, I graduated in the bottom 25 percent of my high school class and failed my second semester of college with an astoundingly embarrassing 0.8 GPA. That's right. I failed nearly every single class. You couldn't find a worse student than me. I was unorganized and undisciplined. I overslept and missed class regularly, and when I was present, I did little to nothing to make use of my class time.

So, how did I go from *that* kid to a dean's list student? How did I go on to gain acceptance into one of the most prestigious academic institutions for graduate school? How did I develop the drive and focus to then start two businesses and travel the world as a speaker and leadership consultant? It's actually a crazy story, and I am honored to be able to tell it.

I'll share more about my story in the next section, but the most pivotal moment in my transformation happened when I changed my major to psychology and discovered my passion for learning how the human mind works. Since then, I've devoted my life to becoming an expert on learning, behavior, and leadership in order to develop the very specific expertise of manifesting greatness in others. I want to share the euphoria I experienced when I broke out of the echo chamber of other people's voices that I had chosen to adopt as my own thoughts. The moment when your journey to self-actualization begins will be the greatest moment in your life. And I have even better news for you: every moment that follows it will top the former (with just a few exceptions). Each moment thereafter will be your new best moment. Once you reach that psychological stage where you have a growth mindset, a sense of purpose, and a taste of self-actualization, you will even learn to see adversity as a blessing. I've grown to learn that adversity is advantageous because resistance is required to build strength.

When I travel and speak to colleges and universities around the globe, my message is always the same: *if college is the best four years of your life, you did it wrong*. College is supposed to be your best time *yet*. And if you do it right, you will have the best four years of your life while setting up your future to continue improving in perpetuity.

Each year after college should be better than the four years you spent in school. This book will walk you through the process of making that happen. Not only does it include an abundance of pertinent information, but it also includes questions for you to ponder, prompts for guided reflection and journaling, and actionable steps you can start taking *today* that will begin preparing your mindset for an enlightening experience like no other. This is not just a novel or textbook, it is a life-changing workbook that will empower you to write your life's story alongside mine, in the hope that you can create your own version of success and happiness, as you choose to define those terms.

My Story

Every photographer will tell you that the setting and the camera lens are two of the most important elements to consider when trying to capture a high-quality photograph. Well, before I can expect you to trust me to help guide you through this journey, I know it is essential that I tell you more about the setting and the lens through which I have come to discover the insights I'm sharing in this book.

As I mentioned in the previous section, college was a transformational experience for me, and it created the foundation for the work I'm doing today, where I help others—like yourself—create their own transformational college years. But before I could reach that transformation, I had to face some challenges. I was that gifted kid in high school who somehow graduated in the bottom 25 percent of my class. Every school has at least one of them…that was me. I was accepted into college almost solely based on my SAT scores and my extracurriculars. While I was not a great student, I was an athlete and active community servant, even from a young age. In hindsight, that was kind of a miracle in and of itself because I didn't care to study or prepare for the SATs. In fact, I took the SATs as a freshman, just to see if I could get a higher score than my older brother, who was a senior. By the time I took the SATs again as a junior, my score had barely changed. I had wasted all four years of my high school education. While I was an idiot for doing that, I was smart enough to know not to apply directly to the school of engineering because I knew I would have most likely been rejected due to my grades. Instead, I started college with an undecided major, with the intention of taking an engineering course load and then transferring into the program at the end of my freshman year.

But within the first month of classes, my faculty adviser from the school of engineering called me into her office. I thought this was just standard procedure. Shortly after I sat down, I realized this was not a normal meeting between an adviser and their advisee. She started off by saying something to the effect of, "I'm not sure why you're here. I don't usually have undecided students, or any students with a high school transcript like yours. Do you have any idea what you are getting yourself into?" I was caught a bit off guard because it suddenly dawned on me that she had seen right through me, before she'd even met me. She knew exactly what kind of student I was, one of the approximate 67 percent who would enter—but would not graduate from—the engineering program at Widener University. She immediately requested that I be transferred to another adviser to save herself the time of dealing with me. She may not have used those exact words, but her message was very clear.

Ouch.

When the time came, I proved her right. I failed miserably. I am ashamed to admit that I received a 0.8 GPA in my second semester. Yes, you read that correctly. I failed every single class except for one—I received a D in that class. In the ensuing meeting with my next adviser (and my mom), I was given two choices: switch majors or leave. I accepted the option to continue school and switch majors because I wasn't ready to give up. The fact that I was nineteen years old and my mom was still coming to my school to meet with my adviser regarding my performance and my behavior really lit a fire under me. At that moment, I realized that my life had to change.

And by my life, I meant *me. I* had to change. I was conscious of the fact that I was an underachiever; this wasn't news to me. But I'd always thought that, when the time came, when the stakes were high, I would suddenly be able to flip a switch and become the high performer I knew I was capable of being. I learned the hard way that this wasn't true. Failing to prepare is preparing to fail, and that is exactly what I did. My habits needed an overhaul, which had to start with my mentality and attitude.

I spent another year undecided, only this time I had zero plan for what I would study afterward. I started taking general education classes while trying to find my passion and learn more about myself. I spent a year reflecting on my life and trying to understand how I had fallen so low and what I'd have to do to get to where I wanted to be. At the time, I didn't quite know where that was, so this was a difficult task.

Toward the end of my first semester as an undecided student, after failing and having numerous wake-up calls, I took a psychology class and was fascinated by it, so I started signing up for more classes during my second semester as an undecided student. I fell in love with the topic when I took my first neuroscience course and learned about the concept called synaptic plasticity. I'll explain it in more detail in the next chapter, but essentially, it's your brain's ability to change itself. People often think of a brain as being like a computer, hardwired to perform certain tasks, but that is not the case. Imagine if your computer could rewire itself to perform better. Imagine a city where the roads could redesign themselves and add lanes to the busiest highways without the need for a construction crew. Your brain invests in its own infrastructure by increasing the capacity of neurons that are the most active. That is what your brain does, every single day.

At the end of my second semester as an undecided student—my fourth semester in total—I had to choose a major in order to move forward. The choice was a no-brainer. *(Ha!)* I didn't find it odd at all that I chose to major in psychology, but everyone else was shocked. I had always been fascinated by abstract concepts, and I was always a great problem-solver, so it made sense to me, but I still received the response you would expect: "You went from engineering to psychology?!" You should have seen the look on my dad's face… But despite the disbelief from others, I knew that psychology was the right fit because I wanted to learn about what motivates people—what drives people—so that I could find out what I was lacking. I wanted to understand the minds and behaviors of others because I'd never understood my own.

Once I found something I wanted to learn about, I had to teach myself how to learn. You would think fifteen years of structured education would have taught me how to learn, but that wasn't the case. In fact, this experience made me realize that we don't learn about the learning process at all. When I began studying the science of the learning and development processes, I was alarmed by how the structure of our education system is misaligned with what the research tells us. Today, I share that research and help schools and businesses close the gaps. And I'll be sharing some of that with you in this book, so you can make changes in your own approach to learning.

Once I understood the learning process and had built a system around it, everything started to click for me. I finally had some sense of direction. Even if I didn't know what I wanted to do with my future, I knew what I wanted to learn about in the moment, and that was enough for me. After a year in psychology, I narrowed my focus on the neurobiology of leadership and motivational behaviors. Of course, that wasn't a major, so not only did I have to excel in the classroom, but I also began educating myself on my own time. I made the dean's list every semester thereafter. After noticing my own transformation, I realized I wanted to devote my life to helping others realize their potential. I wanted to do so by helping them find their passion and achieve monumental success, but most importantly, I wanted to guide them toward discovering their true significance. (We will differentiate success from significance in a later chapter.)

In this book, I will elaborate on the steps I took to develop from the passionless, underachieving, and lackluster student to the mentor I am today among academic and business leaders alike. This book started as a note to my freshman self. From there, it unfolded into a document where I dumped all of the most important lessons I had learned in college that I wanted to carry with me forever. Ultimately, it all became too powerful to keep to myself.

Before I share what I know, I want to acknowledge what I don't know. I humbly accept that, as you read this book, there will be questions that will come to your mind which I will fail to answer in these pages. With this book, you are not just getting a series of stories (both painful and comical), and you are not just reviewing a compilation of psychological research findings that will allow you to maximize your potential. You are also receiving my eternal loyalty and support. You have officially become a part of my story. You are holding my first book, the manifestation of every ounce of value I could synthesize into words on this subject. As you read, please write down every question you have, and then cross them off if they are answered later in the book. If you reach the end of the book and still have any unanswered questions, I implore you to reach out to me and I will search relentlessly with you to find the answers. Because you are holding this book (whether it is a digital or paper copy), you have me as your companion to walk along this journey with you, and I hope you will take advantage of that opportunity. My success story will be worthless to me if it does not inspire others, like yourself, to change their lives for the better.

I've been blessed with a unique name, so I am easy to find on social media. My handle is the same on every platform: @dantedibattista. You can also find my direct contact information on my website at https://dantedibattista.com/. You can also ask me questions through my podcast, *The Pursuit of Self-Actualization*, which has been distinguished globally as one of the top podcasts in the education category. There is this cool feature on Anchor (where I host the podcast) that allows you to record voice messages and send them to me. I can use your voice message and dedicate an entire episode to helping you explore the solutions to your questions. Visit https://anchor.fm/tpsa to submit a voice message. You can also find the show on Spotify, Apple iTunes, or any other major podcast platform.

Alright, enough about me…now let's talk about you. You may be one of those students who graduated near the top of your class in high school. If you are, I applaud you. This book contains lessons that will help you carry that academic success through college. But, while academic success is vital for graduating college, that isn't the only important part of the college experience. And so, this book will also model what success looks like beyond the classroom, on campus and in your personal life. I want you to know, I had friends in college who excelled in class, and some of them laughed at me when I failed. It was an external source of validation for them to believe that they were better than me in some way. They carried that validation across the stage as they graduated on time (a year before me). But, in some cases, that stage was where that validation ended. I graduated a year later, but I found a job before some of those same friends had. Years later, it seems like their growth ended after they graduated. I will share those stories with you as well. The point is: while academics are absolutely essential, they are actually a much smaller part of the college experience than you (and most others) realize.

If my story resonated with you, if you are one of the students who struggled to get through high school and are petrified of failing out of college, don't worry. I assure you that I will help you establish a sense of confidence. This book will show you step-by-step instructions on how to build habits that will set you up for success. I've had the privilege of interviewing some of the top performers in the world, including Olympic gold medalists, best-selling authors, and multimillionaire entrepreneurs, and many of them started out like you and me. You are right where you need to be, in the pages of this book.

This book also highlights critical issues that exist on college campuses across the country, and the lies you were told about the college experience. I will point out the traps that have been set that can cause you to fall into holes you couldn't have imagined existed.

I hope you read this book carefully, reflect on the stories along the way, and laugh at my past misery as much as I have. It was truly a wild ride, so buckle up.

Warning:

The concepts you are about to read about are simple to explain but difficult to implement. Be patient with yourself and trust the process. As you navigate this book, pause to take notes and reflect on how the concepts apply to you. Be creative as we begin to navigate the strategic planning of your future for college and beyond. Don't try to do things my way; try to do them *your* way.

This book is meant to be a series of sparks, and it is up to you to bring the fuel for the fire. I can't do the work for you. A personal trainer can write the perfect diet and workout program for you, but reading it won't produce results. The only way to manifest success is through your habits. As Mahatma Gandhi once said,

Your beliefs become your thoughts,
Your thoughts become your words,
Your words become your actions,
Your actions become your habits,
Your habits become your values,
Your values become your destiny.

That is where this journey begins…with your beliefs and your thoughts.

Step 1: Develop the Right Mindset

In order to help you develop the right mindset, you first need to believe that you are in total control of it—no one and nothing can influence your mindset *unless you allow them to*. To help illustrate this fact, let's look first at the scientific discipline of metacognition, and then I'll help you apply those concepts practically, in your everyday life. Metacognition is, in the simplest of terms, the process of thinking about your own thinking. If you begin to analyze your thought processes so that you can understand how they work and the forces that influence them, you can then identify and manipulate those forces in your life. Once you start the process of manipulating your environment, you can observe the outcomes and begin adjusting the stimuli around you, like you would in a chemistry experiment, to find the perfect concoction that will continuously provide what you want or need. Think of your brain and your behavior like a feedback loop, because that's exactly how it works.

The initial presentation of this "feedback loop" theoretical approach to behavior is known as cybernetics, and it has been used to invent various technological marvels, such as target-locking missiles. Think about how a target-locking missile works. It identifies an object and then follows it. It uses sensory information to see if the object is moving, calculates the trajectory of the moving object, and then calculates how it needs to adjust its own trajectory to meet that moving object. Then it performs that adjustment through whatever propelling mechanism it has available, and it repeats the process thousands of times per second until it eventually hits its target. This is the level of targeting and redirecting you'll learn to do when it comes to your own life.

The Feedback Loop

The basic concept is that your behavior is driven by your goals, standards, or expectations in the same way as the target-locking missile explained above. You create a goal—or a reference value—completely free from what is occurring around you; it exists solely in your mind. You may justify that reference value with evidence you have acquired from your environment, but in the end, it exists within you, and you have control over it. You set this goal just like you would program a missile. You tell the missile where to go, and it finds its way. You do the same thing with your goal: you determine your destination, and then it's up to you to get yourself there.

Now, you may disagree with me here because maybe your parents raised you to believe you must become a doctor, and that is your "only" choice. Well, that's false; you *do* have other choices. You may choose to follow that path because you want to make your parents happy, you want to be successful, and you want to help people. That choice still followed this same process. You made a calculated choice to follow their guidance because you weighed the pros and cons.

However, our culture and our values determine the weights of various things in our lives. People who grew up in individualistic cultures (like Western cultures) tend to give less weight to the opinions of their family members when making decisions. There has been neuroscience research that highlights this. The researchers asked people from different parts of the world to talk about their relationships with their families, while the participants were connected to a brain scanner. The researchers discovered that, in certain parts of the world, when people talked about themselves, the same part of the brain lit up as when they were talking about their family. In other words, their brain did not distinguish a difference on a biological level between their individual identity and their family. While they were using different words, the two were treated as one in the same. While the weight and importance of feeling pride from one's parents varies across cultures, it is common across cultures to want proud parents, so we are going to stick with that example.

You want to have proud parents—that is the goal—and you are making the choice to become a doctor because you believe it will bring you closer to that reference value of having proud parents. As a result of this internal choice, you begin to make decisions to interact with your external environment in such a way that will match you internal goal or reference value. If you are a visual learner, I encourage you to google "cybernetic theory diagram" to find a visual representation of the concept I am walking you through.

Following this same example, if being a doctor is what you believe will make you happy, and you're not a doctor yet, you are **comparing** your current situation to your **goal** or **reference value** and noticing a discrepancy. What do you do? You think about why you're not a doctor yet, and you conclude that, to be a doctor, you must have a medical degree. As a result, that is what you will choose to pursue. Just like the missile, you've used the propelling mechanisms at your disposal to move your current position toward your desired position. Your brain processes the goal and identifies what is missing from your current situation that separates you from that goal, and it produces **behaviors**—or an **output function**—that are intended to close that gap. Your brain then uses your senses to observe the result by assessing the **effect on your environment**. Is your behavior bringing you closer to or farther from your goal? Was there an **external disturbance** that interrupted your behavior that you hadn't expected? When you're using a GPS and you arrive at a road that is closed for construction, the GPS is then forced to reroute you toward your destination. Your brain does the same rerouting. It processes the information you've gathered about your environment (and any external disturbances) as **input functions** and connects those back into your decision-making mechanisms—and the cycle continues. This occurs thousands of times a day; in fact, some studies suggest we make approximately thirty-five thousand decisions per day (Daum 2012). So, by teaching you strategies to analyze and improve your decision-making process, I am giving you the chance to make your life thirty-five thousand times better each and every day. (I really should have charged way more for this book!)

The beautiful part about this entire process is that you are not hard-

wired like a missile or a GPS. You have control over all four of the main components in your internal decision-making system:
1) The goal
2) The metric (or comparator) you use to determine your success
3) Your behavior (or the output function)
4) How you perceive your environment (or your input function)

Goal

This is why being goal-oriented is seen as such a desirable trait by employers, family members, and friends alike. People like being around other people who set goals, communicate them, and deliver on them. Do you have that one friend who talks a big game but never follows through? How much do you really enjoy spending time with that friend? Your frustration comes from the misalignment between the expectations they set and the reality their behavior produces. I used to be that friend, and many people in my life during that transformational experience would attest to that. If you are this person, understand that you are extremely frustrating to be around sometimes. Everyone around you sees the potential in you and wants to watch you reach it. Reward their belief in you by delivering, because if you don't, you will be surround by people who doubt you—and you will begin to internalize that doubt. They are not wrong for doubting you; you are wrong for giving them reason to. As we continue through this book, I will help you communicate your goals in a more effective way, and I'll help you manage the expectations of others without losing your ability to dream big and deliver in a sustainable way that keeps the dreams flowing and keeps the supportive people in your life.

If you're not that friend, because you always follow through, that is truly something to be proud of and build on. Use that foundation to begin setting larger goals with broader implications, and continue to deliver those results. However, you should also be aware of how much power you are giving away if you're allowing the satisfaction of others to dictate your own happiness. That is something that belongs to you, not to them. I have a podcast episode on

The Pursuit of Self-Actualization, entitled "How to Be Selflessly Selfish," where I talk about this. We always tell people that they can't pour from an empty cup, but we don't teach people how to build a coffee maker. If you are always following through on promises, pouring from your cup to fill the cups of others, without building a life that fills your cup for you, it will eventually run dry, with nothing left over for you. And if you're not careful, you will surround yourself with people who only want what is in your cup—and those kinds of people won't be there for you when you no longer have anything to pour into theirs.

Comparator

The second component, the comparator, plays an important role in your well-being. There is no way around the fact that we are social creatures with an innate desire to compare ourselves to others and perceive ourselves through the lenses of others. Let's approach this from an evolutionary psychology per-spective. At its core, the science of evolutionary psychology (Downes and Zalta 2021) is rather simple. It is a field of study that conducts research based on the premise that our behaviors are manifestations of what helped our ancestors survive.

One thing I have always found fascinating is the human tendency to separate ourselves from the animal kingdom, as if we are outside observers of it and not a product of it all the same. The fact of the matter is, we are animals. If you take a step back to objectively observe human behavior from this perspective and see how we evolved to be this way, you can start to make choices about how to handle your own behavior. You can start asking yourself questions like: *How did this serve my ancestors, and does it still serve me the same way?* You may start to notice that not everything your ancestors needed to survive applies to you anymore.

This social desirability component of human behavior *definitely* still serves you, just not in the same way it once served your ancestors. Let me explain. Before we had technology such as refrigerators to safely store food, or the understanding of how farming worked, our ancestors were hunters and gatherers. You probably learned about that in grade school, so I won't go much further, but let's look at that history from a different perspective. What did that period mean for us in a psychological sense? Well, it caused us to be extremely reliant upon each other. Groups of people would go out and hunt, and maybe they would come back with something. If they came back with something, it was not advantageous to hoard it because you couldn't store it, anyway. There was no such thing as an accumulation of wealth because our ancestors from that period only had each other, the resources available at the moment, and the drive to live. Social status was acquired through catching something for the entire tribe or village to eat. (The argument can be made that this was where our desire to host people for feasts came from, and why social status has been associated with the ability to be a quality host.)

Millennia have passed since this stage of human evolution, and yet we are still so focused on the opinions of those in our perceived tribe. Sometimes it is hard to notice because, in many ways, we still grow up isolated within certain tribes or groups, such as our family, our church, and the kids who grew up in the same school district as us. But the reality is, we have a freedom our ancestors could have never dreamed of. Yet, we hear their whispers in the back of our mind telling us to follow the tribe.

When you hear those comparator voices or have those inclinations, the first thing you should do is show gratitude to those voices because they are the reason you were born. Without those voices, your ancestors would have starved, and your genes would not have been passed down to you. But once you take a moment to show gratitude, move on from them. You live in a world where you can choose which comparators to pay attention to. You can choose your own tribe, one that supports you for who you want to be, not for the version of yourself they want you to be to affirm their own insecurities.

There was a reason why I used the earlier example of parents who want you to be a doctor. Many of our parents are guilty of passing on to us a scarcity mindset that drives their desire for us to pursue certain markers of success, like becoming a doctor. But it is ironic. Our parents and grandparents worked incredibly hard to give us opportunities and freedoms they did not have, and they are quick to remind us of that. Yet, when we want to use those opportunities and freedoms to pursue a version of happiness they could not have experienced due to their own scarcity or lack of security, they try to stop us. Those are the voices of their ancestors, whom they've never met, whispering in their ears. But that is not what they truly want for you. They want you to be happy, they want to live vicariously through you. They want to watch you blossom into the version of themselves they had turned away from when they were faced with uncertainty. If you want to become a doctor, *go for it*! Please, go all in, and I am happy to help you as much as I can along the way. However, if you know you will be much happier doing something else, and you are only doing this to make your family proud in the short term, you are setting up your relationship with your parents for failure in the long term. You run the risk of building a foundation of resentment in your relationship. What if you become a doctor, only to realize that you are unhappy with your choice and that you did it for your parents? You will find yourself blaming them for your unhappiness when it was *you* who chose that path in the first place. The unfortunate truth is, one day, the people in our lives will pass, and we will be stuck with the results of our decisions. You are the only one who is guaranteed to be here for your entire life, so your voice should be the one you pay the most attention to.

The best example I've ever heard for this came from Kerwin Rae's interview on his show, *Unstoppable*, when he was interviewing a guest by the name of Vinh Giang. Vinh is now a world-renowned magician, but he started his career as an accountant. He had a safe, steady, lucrative job that he was good at—something every parent wants for their kid. However, what makes Vinh's story different is that he loved doing magic tricks. Every day after work, he would do tricks for the people in the various departments within the company. One of the partners, who had started and built the company, watched Vinh from a distance, until one day, he decided to approach Vinh.

The partner told Vinh, "In six months' time, one of two things is going to happen. I am either going to fire you, or you can quit."

Vinh was shocked, confused, and immediately afraid that his father would kill him when he found out Vinh had lost his job. As Vinh proceeded to tell the story on the podcast, he shared how he remembered that partner of the company because he always used to walk around with one hand in his pocket, and Vinh always found that kind of strange. Well, after the partner told him what was going to happen in six months' time, he pulled his hand out of his pocket to show Vinh the bad arthritis in that hand.

He told Vinh, "I love playing the piano. I gave it up when I was in my late twenties to build this firm. I had the opportunity to play in orchestras all over the world. I gave that up to build this. I'd give this all up. I'd trade you my car, all my wealth, to have your youth again to make the right decision. I can never play piano again. You need to do what you love; you're in the wrong career."

Naturally, Vinh's biggest fear was how his parents would respond.

So, Vinh asked the partner, "Can you come home and tell my dad the same thing you just told me?"

And sure enough, the partner did.

By doing that, Vinh said,

> He helped my dad see something in me that my dad was afraid to see. My dad knew that I had "magical" talents, but he was afraid to see it. My dad has known so much adversity in his life that, to him, he clung to security. Whereas doing what you love is something that my dad never had the luxury of being able to do. Because of that fear. And so, he helped my dad see something. My dad already knew I had this, but that night, my dad was able to put fear aside. Because someone else who was successful in his eyes, validated his son.

From that day on, Vinh's parents were his biggest fans. After that dinner, and after that realization, Vinh's dad told him something that Vinh would never forget.

He said, "Son, look, you owe me one thing; you know this, boy. You actually owe me one thing. You have to jump as high as you can in this life. And as long as I'm alive, I'll forever be your net from this point on."

The reason I went on that detour for a moment is to highlight the importance of your comparator. You have control over it, even when others try to determine it for you.

Self-Actualization: The One True Comparator

The fact of the matter is that the comparator should be the same for everyone: self-actualization. That won't look the same for everyone, but at the end of the day, that is the one true metric we must use.

If you're not familiar with what self-actualization means or where the term comes from, it is what Abraham Maslow labeled as the highest level of what he called the hierarchy of needs in his theory of human motivation. It describes the need to pursue the fulfillment of your potential rather than the pursuit of other, more superficial goals such as obtaining material wealth, popularity, or esteem. However, it is impossible to be motivated to do anything if your basic survival needs and your need for security are unfulfilled.

From bottom to top, the order of the hierarchy goes like this:
1) Psychological needs
2) Safety needs
3) Love and belonging
4) Esteem
5) Self-actualization

If you google Maslow's hierarchy of needs, you will see that motivation is like a pyramid, and it first requires a strong foundation. Each level depends on the one below it to be sustainable. You can also use this theory to see why seeking the approval of others will never allow you to achieve the ultimate forms of happiness and success. It traps you in the phases of love and belonging or esteem. You will never be able to become the most you can be—as you define it—by focusing on the opinions of others.

The desire to serve others because you are driven to do so is worlds apart from confining yourself within the parameters of someone else's expectations. Be the best you can be, so that those people you care about can have the best brother, sister, son, daughter, friend, husband, wife, mother, father, cousin, or whatever you may be to them.

This version of self-actualization that I have chosen to adopt, which differs slightly from what is taught in psychology programs around the world, can be traced back to when Abraham Maslow visited the Siksika people of the Blackfoot Confederacy in the summer of 1938 (Ravilochan 2021). There is documentation that shows that this visit had molded Maslow's idea of self-actualization into the version we discuss today. Many of the self-proclaimed self-help gurus out there will portray self-actualization as the pursuit to maximize yourself for your own gain, which is not the case. The Siksika tribe determined the status hierarchy based on who gave away the most and accumulated the least. It is rooted in the understanding that we exist to serve each other, and in order to do that effectively, we ourselves must be fulfilled. This goes back to the analogy regarding pouring from an empty cup.

Output Function

This is where the output function, or your behavior, comes into play. You changed your focus to only compare your current position to the ideal version of yourself, the version that can do the most good for the most people in the world around you while remaining fulfilled. Now what? You work backward. You reverse engineer your own development by focusing on what the ideal version of yourself looks like and the behaviors required to produce that outcome. Then you plan your day around producing those behaviors. And you keep score. Every morning, I try to set goals and reflect. And every evening, I measure my success in achieving those goals. I've become my own coach.

Now, changing your behavior revolves around the idea of improving every single day. It doesn't really matter what it is you want to improve; that is your business. What matters is that you are focusing on growth. You start analyzing your own behavior differently. The math is simple:

$$\text{Your current self: } (1.00)^{365} = 1.00$$
$$\text{Your current self, plus 1\% daily growth: } (1.01)^{365} = 37.78$$

If you focus on getting 1 percent better every day, the compounding effects are massive. One year of your life (365 days) devoted to growth will make you nearly 38 times the person you are right now. And imagine if you do that for four (or five) years during your college experience. Furthermore, imagine continuing that process after graduation and early in your career. Imagine how far that will take you!

Effect on Environment

You'll notice that, as your behavior and demeanor change, so will the environment around you. People will treat you differently, you will see yourself differently, opportunities you never considered before will present themselves to you, and you'll have to decide for yourself if the changes in your environment match the outcomes you were looking for. Are you attracting new people into your life whom you don't want? That could represent a sign that you're heading in the wrong direction. Are you finding yourself in positions you originally did not intend to be in? That could indicate that your ideas about the outcomes your changes would bring were set under false pretenses.

Going through this process will train you to observe the impact you have on the environment around you. This will become an extremely important skill as you move forward in life. When I became a leader within student organizations on campus, I found myself to be a very vocal leader. That is not necessarily a good or bad thing, it's just a general observation. I am a talker by nature. I'm an author, a podcast host, and a public speaker by trade—this is no surprise to me or to anyone who knows me.

However, one of the most important leadership lessons I've ever learned was to prioritize building self-awareness. So, I decided to occasionally attend meetings while remaining in complete silence. I would not speak up until I was directly asked. I evaluated the impact the absence of my voice created in the room. Did anyone speak up who would normally take my place as the silent member in the room? How often did people directly ask me to speak up? Once I noticed there were people in the room who originally did not have the opportunity to speak because of my presence, I made it my intention to directly ask for their input in future meetings when I was speaking. Taking a moment to sit back and analyze how changes in my behavior impacted the environment around me allowed me to generate insights about my role within the group.

It also taught me another powerful lesson: there were rooms where my voice was heard but not welcomed. When I stopped talking, no one checked in. When I did talk, people listened just enough to formulate their rejection responses. If your presence does not impact the room you are in, you must decide whether how you carry yourself must change or if you must choose a different room. I found this choice to be a challenging one because the room where you are least likely to generate an impact is often the room that needs your influence the most.

While most of my focus has been on the impact of behavior on our external environment, the term *environment* can also include your headspace, i.e., your mental health. We often say that you must see something to believe it, but the inverse is also true: you must believe in something to see it. If you begin experimenting with your routines, for example, and you only stick with the changes for one day, you probably won't see any results. But if you stick with them for a few weeks, believing they will eventually have an impact, they have a higher probability of producing the results you were looking for. If you decide you want to lose weight, go to the gym once, work incredibly hard, and eat the smallest salad you've ever eaten in your life, and you expect to wake up the next day with abs, you are inevitably going to be disappointed.

The internal monologue you have with yourself is an ecosystem where certain thoughts and behaviors are contingent upon each other. Because the brain operates as a chemical feedback loop, every thought simultaneously serves as the response of a chemical reaction and the trigger for another one. So, how does your mental health respond to the experiments? Do you find yourself having a more positive outlook? Do you find that you have more energy? Do you find that you sleep better?

Therefore, what I am teaching you is how to treat yourself like a psychology experiment. Every time I find myself being critical of my habits or performance in some way, I ask myself where the criticism is coming from and whether it is valid—and if it is valid, I take specific actions to address it. I come up with potential solutions, experiment, and document the journey. If I believe a change in my habits will lead me to sleep better, I need to keep a sleep log, document my current baseline, manipulate my routine, and then see if I notice a change in my sleep logs. Do I wake up less? Do I fall asleep earlier? Do I wake up easier? Learning how to design your life with intention, to heighten your sense of self-awareness, and to create systems that help you maximize your opportunities to find fulfillment and share it with others will allow you to not only have a transformational college experience, but it will also help you lead transformations within every community where you are a member.

Input Function

In the world of target-locking missiles, an input function is a form of sensory input. Are you closer to your target or not? It is measured by distance. While that is also true for the brain, in the physical world, it can be more abstract than that. How do you measure whether the changes you are making are effective in an environment that is not concrete? To continue from my previous example, I observed how my change in behavior impacted the behaviors of those around me. This was not as straightforward as measuring the distance between two objects. I can't pull out a ruler during a meeting and measure behavioral changes among my colleagues. However, I can count how often certain people speak during a meeting and then manipulate the only variable I can control, which is myself, to see how my changes cause other people to behave. I can then analyze the delta, or difference, and come to conclusions based on what I see.

The input function is critical to your success. I mentioned before that we have the concept of belief backward: we say you must see something to believe it, but it is also true that we must believe in something to truly see it.

How we choose to digest the information available in the world around us will determine how we respond to it. You can fail a test and see that as a reflection of your capabilities and who you are, leading to a sense of defeat and depression. Or you can view failure as an opportunity to learn and grow, which will empower you to change your strategy and try again. It is important to understand that the results the world returns to you are not a reflection of you but a reflection of how you are interacting with the world around you.

If I set a goal to sleep better, and I do research that tells me drinking lemon juice before bed will help and it doesn't, does that mean something is wrong with me? No, it means I searched for information and trusted the wrong source. The next step is for me to figure out what sources I should trust and how I can identify them. Many people give up because they try strategies that had little to no opportunity to succeed, and then they see the failure as a reflection of their inability to achieve the desired result, rather than a reflection of the strategy they selected.

This is the part of the journey where you must call into question your worldview and what shapes it. Here is what that looked like for me: I've noticed in myself a tendency to play out scenarios in my head prior to any altercation. If I think I have to deliver bad news to someone, I imagine all of the ways it can go wrong. I play out the argument in my head repeatedly. I think of all the things the other person is going to say about me, and I find myself emotionally responding to them. I can be alone in a room, upset about something that no one said in a conversation that has not yet taken place. I do this to myself all the time. When I identified this behavior and decided I wanted to change it, I had to figure out why it exists in the first place. Every behavior is a form of communication. What was this habit communicating to me?

It made me realize that I have an unhealthy relationship with conflict. I see conflict as a bad thing, something to avoid and prepare for. I treated conflict like a battle, and the war going on in my mind was my boot camp. This means that I treated anyone with whom I had conflict as an enemy to defeat, and I assumed they would treat me the same. As a result, I was aggressive in my approach toward conflict, which caused others to respond in the same way, and suddenly, the conflicts would escalate. This reaffirmed my belief that conflict, by nature, would always escalate into a battle. This was a self-fulfilling prophecy that I had accepted as a universal truth. I learned instead that conflict is healthy, when handled appropriately. In fact, conflict is a good thing. Conflict means you have more than one option. Have you ever been stuck in a situation where you only have one choice, and it's not a good one? I would rather be in a situation where I'm discussing which option is the best rather than a situation where no option worth debating is available.

I later adopted a philosophy that I share with everyone with whom I anticipate I will have conflict: it is not you versus me; it is us versus the problem. I learned that conflict creates opportunity for collaboration, which means that I have an opportunity to learn from others and accomplish things greater than what I am able to accomplish on my own. Now I teach conflict resolution courses to leaders in some of the most high-stress environments around the world. I encourage you to adopt a similar approach when you inevitably experience conflict with your friends, family, or college faculty and staff members.

The Power of the Feedback Loop

That example highlights the power of the feedback loop. It has tremendous power, particularly over your self-esteem. If you are pursuing a goal with an idea of what success looks like in your mind, and you're trying relentlessly to make it happen but you're not getting any closer, it can destroy your confidence. You can start to feel powerless and might tell yourself, *it doesn't matter what I do, I can't do it.* That thought process leads to inaction, which creates an environment that acts as a perpetual reminder that you are nowhere near where you want to be, and you can't do anything about it. This thought-process paralysis is the result of a negative feedback loop. If you ever feel like this, or you are approaching this place mentally, you must stop and reflect on all four components of the feedback loop and start making changes.

For those of you who may be reading this and are feeling the frustration of the big societal issues that plague our communities and your desire to change them, I applaud you. However, in order to make an impact for others, you must first focus on becoming the best version of yourself, so you can then support your initiatives and drive change. Feeling overwhelmed by the weight and magnitude of the problem won't help you lift it. It's cliché, but instead of wishing the path was easier, focus on developing the strength to overcome it.

Think of the greatest changemakers in history. They all focused on developing the skills needed to mobilize an army of supporters to drive change. If you have similar aspirations, you will need to focus on developing those same communication skills. The goal then becomes the consistent and intentional development of those skills. That is a tangible goal that brings you closer to your greater goal without crumbling under the weight of your own ambition. And the power to do that lies in understanding the feedback loop you are operating within and redefining each phase of it to produce the outcomes you are looking for.

Whenever I approach a problem that I am unable to solve, I always think of it this way: First, I ask myself what I would have to be capable of in order to overcome the problem. Then, I imagine what that version of myself would look like. What would my life be like? How would I be able to impact those I care most about? If the result is worth the sacrifice—which it always is, in the pursuit of self-actualization—I idolize that version of myself. I never compare myself to others; instead, I compare who I am now to the person I want to be tomorrow, and that is it.

You may have heard Matthew McConaughey's famous acceptance speech from the Oscars in 2014 and are now thinking that this philosophy sounds familiar, and you would be right. He talked about who his hero is, and how his answer is always the same: himself, in ten years. The constant process of imagining a better version of yourself, and pursuing that relentlessly, is the best and most effective way to live a happy and fulfilling life.

However, that is much easier said than done. The process requires a focus on being uncomfortable, and it requires self-awareness. It requires that you address the insecurities you don't want to address because avoiding them is easier than dealing with the pain they cause you. I'm here to tell you that you deserve better from yourself. You are worthy of your own unconditional love and support. Treat yourself the way you would treat the person you love most in this world. You don't deserve to have those triggers haunt you. If you don't know where or what those triggers are yet, the college experience will find a way to bring them out of you. And that is one of the best parts of the experience, if you do it right.

> The definition of hell is: Your last day on Earth, the person you became meets the person you could have become.
> —Dan Sullivan, *Who Not How*

The Power of Your Brain

As you begin to perceive the world through the lens of metacognition, you may come to the same realization I did, which is that many of the greatest technological feats were the result of humans simply recreating certain elements of ourselves. Pause and reflect on this for a moment. If you had to pick a superpower, any superpower, what would it be? Chances are that humans are already doing it to some capacity. X-ray vision? Thousands of x-rays are conducted around the world every day. The ability to fly? You can buy a plane ticket. Want to have super speed? Drive a Porsche. Want to read minds? Scroll through someone's Facebook feed or TikTok FYP. The ability to resurrect the dead? We have home movies to watch and relive the most precious moments with the most precious people in our lives. We invented cameras by recreating the eyeball; we just added a pause button. We invented mechanical brains in the form of computers that can remember the things we forget. We studied the immune system and created vaccines. Being human is as close to being supernatural as it gets.

I hope that, by the end of this book, I will have convinced you that the brain you are using to process this information is the most powerful tool in existence, and that your ability to use it can overcome even the greatest challenges. But just like any other tool, it is only as good as the ability of the one using it. Ironically, though, your brain is the architect of the person using it, and your experiences rewire your brain, changing the architecture of your self-perception and how you see the world around you.

That's right. We are not 100 percent hardwired. Contrary to popular belief, the brain does, in fact, change. It can reroute neural pathways when parts of your brain die; for example, if you lose a digit, the brain region responsible for the sensory information of that digit can be taken over and used for other purposes—your brain can adjust. And this ability goes beyond sensory information. It's truly marvelous, if you think about it. The brain's ability to change and rewire itself is known as synaptic plasticity. Synapses are the spaces between your brain cells where chemical messages are transmitted. Plasticity describes the adaptability of an organism. Think of the way plastic materials are malleable; your brain is the same way.

Yes, we have genetic dispositions and tendencies we've inherited from our ancestors, but that does not mean our behaviors are set in stone. In fact, even our genes have the ability to change how they are expressed through epigenetics. Think of your DNA like a book…a very long book. Epigenetics describes how experiences can change the way that book is read. It won't rewrite the book or your genetic code, but there may be a chapter your parents never read but passed on to you that will be opened as a result of experiences. We have an incredible ability to change based on our experiences. Since we have free will, we can make choices to create experiences that have been put to the test via the scientific method and have produced results. In this book, I am going to walk you through those experiments, what they mean, and how you can apply them to your own college experience and make it transformational, in the same way I did. Together, you and I are going to create a vision for your "best self" and draw a road map from who you are today to the person you want to become through your college experience. This book doesn't come with all of the answers. Instead, it comes with empowering lessons, thought-provoking research, and questions that dive deeply into the root of all the obstacles that stand in your way so you can dismantle and overcome them. There are many forms of synaptic plasticity, but the form we are going to be referring to is known as long-term potentiation, or LTP. "LTP is a process that increases the efficiency of synaptic transmission, which is widely believed to be the neural basis of most, if not all, forms of learning and memory" (Costandi 2016). In more common terms, it is the process of your brain changing itself to make it better and quicker at sending messages.

When you look at the anatomy of the brain cell, also known as the neuron, you will see that there are dendrites near the cell body (or the soma). Dendrites are like branches on a tree, but to the neuron, they are the receivers of messages. Your brain has billions of these cells that intertwine and overlap each other. The spaces between them are called synapses. Those spaces are where chemical messages are sent from axons and received by dendrites. This occurs millions of times per second to cause you to do things like move your fingers, and it is what allows you to perceive sensory information like seeing this book, feeling the texture of the paper, and hearing sounds around you.

When you use a certain neural pathway often, your brain notices and starts investing resources into making that pathway stronger and more efficient. Those dendrites grow extra little branches to ensure they can handle receiving more signals and do so more quickly. The axons also begin producing more messenger cells called neurotransmitters. Your brain even begins to move behaviors you perform often closer and closer to the center of your brain so the messages have to travel a shorter distance, further increasing the speed and efficiency. This, in a nutshell, is the process of long-term potentiation, and you can use this form of synaptic plasticity to your advantage when it comes to your perception of yourself.

Your perception of yourself is what is commonly referred to as self-esteem. It is essential that you have a healthy self-perception so that you can believe in your ability to achieve your goals. People underestimate the power of believing in themselves, but belief can play an important role in how your brain functions. One of the greatest examples of this is the placebo effect. If you are anything like me, you need to see evidence, something scientific. Well, science overwhelmingly believes in the placebo effect. If you are unfamiliar with the term, it is often applied in the field of medicine. The introduction to the first chapter of my psychopharmacology textbook (Meyer and Quenzer 2004) tells the story of how the placebo effect was discovered, and I would like to share it with you:

The Italian campaign of World War II involved the Allied invasion of Sicily and the Italian mainland during the period from 1943-1945. The ultimate victory left 60,000 Allied soldiers dead and 320,000 casualties. Among the casualties were American troops who were treated by a Harvard-based anesthesiologist named Henry Beecher. The prolonged intense bombardment by the Germans caused significant shortages of supplies and medications, including those given to relieve pain, such as morphine. Out of that desperate circumstance came a fascinating finding that has generated enormous research since that time. It seems that as supplies of morphine dwindled to nothing, Dr. Beecher's nursing assistant, in an effort to be compassionate, injected the soldiers with saline solution while reassuring them that they were getting the potent painkiller. To her total amazement, she observed that the inert injection dramatically reduced the soldiers' agony and prevented the drop in blood pressure that leads to life-threatening shock. The initial discovery prompted Beecher to return to Harvard after the war and empirically study the healing art of deception as it relates to improved patient care and modern drug testing. Beecher revolutionized how new medications were tested and initiated the use of a placebo group, whose outcome would be compared with that of the group receiving the medication to be tested. At last, there was an impartial way to determine whether the new drug was truly effective.

(One small comment I need to slide in here is that, while Beecher rightfully receives credit for the research he conducted after observing this phenomenon, I want you to pause and think about the fact that one of the most significant discoveries in the history of medicine was brought about by the empathy of a nursing assistant. While you should rightfully feel proud of your accomplishments, also be sure to stop and thank the "nursing assistants" in your life, all of the people who would otherwise fade into the background of history.)

The placebo effect is used to describe the phenomenon in double-blind studies when participants are given a sugar pill but are told they are being given medication (Meyer and Quenzer 2004). Participants in these studies report experiencing relief of the ailments they had expected the medicine would fix.

That's right: if you give someone a sugar pill and tell them it is a pain reliever, they will often experience pain relief. Simply believing you are receiving something, even if that belief is false, is enough to cause your brain to change the signals it is sending. This effect is so powerful that it is the reason double-blind studies are necessary. You see, to test if a drug is effective, researchers must give a group of people a sugar pill and tell them it's the real thing. Researchers must prove that the drug itself is more effective than the sugar pill, i.e., the placebo effect.

Your brain is an incredible tool that sometimes operates in counter-intuitive ways. Who would have thought that deceiving the brain would help it heal pain? Another example of the counterintuitive nature of the brain is our relationship with failure. We fear it, run from it, detest it. Yet, failure is the greatest learning opportunity.

The Importance of Failure

This book started as a note to my freshman self. After I finally graduated, I couldn't help but look back in amazement at all the growth I had experienced and all the resilience I had developed through my adversity. I could barely recognize the young man looking back at me in the mirror, because he was a version of myself that I had never imagined becoming. I was compelled to pause and reflect on my journey to understand how this transformation could have been possible. As I did that, I realized how much wisdom I had gained from my mistakes and how naive I really had been when I had first started college. I wanted to write down all of the things I wished I had known, and I wanted to share that advice with everyone who was going to pursue the journey of self-actualization through their college experience.

Certain things you are going to have to learn through experience. One thing you will notice as you read this book is that most of the wisdom I share (if not all of it) has come from my failures. You are going to fail—somehow, someway—in this process. It is inevitable. I did not write this book to prevent you from failing. I wrote this book to prepare you for failure, and to show you how to practice failing forward, as Denzel Washington once said in his commencement speech at the University of Pennsylvania. This book provides the framework for getting through those failures and manifesting your experiences into exponential growth.

I am about to do for you something that my father did for me at a young age. When I was around fourteen years old, he sat me down in his office and had a brief but stern message for me. It went something like this:

> "Son, this is going to be the last time we have a conversation like this. I'm done. You think for yourself and don't listen to anything your mother or I tell you, so I'm not going to continue wasting my time. Here is how this is going to go moving forward. If you want to be a man so badly, I am not going to get in your way. Just know this: if you ever come to me asking for help that a man wouldn't need, for help that only a boy would need, you won't get any from me. I don't know when it's going to happen—it could be next year, it could be when you turn eighteen, or when you're twenty-five, it may not even happen until you're forty—but *one day*, something will happen and everything I have been trying to tell you will click. I have planted the seed, and it's up to you to let it grow."

Well, he was right. (Don't tell him I said that, though.) It happened when I was nineteen, when I was failing college and my mom had to come to the school to hear about my inability to do what needed to be done—again, as she had done seemingly thousands of times before over the course of my life. My mom has never stopped supporting me. I've tested her patience and have discovered that it is truly endless. While I dearly appreciated her support, it was also more than I deserved. Because my dad was right, it was a waste of her time and energy. I wasn't showing either of my parents the respect they deserved. So, after that happened, I decided to move out of their house and live on my own. I realized that the unconditional support in my home environment had been crippling me. In the real world, nothing in life outside of your family's love (in some cases, if you're really lucky) is unconditional. So I cut myself off from their support and I never asked for a penny again. I tried to do everything on my own. I lived in a run-down row home with two of my friends, and when we moved in, there was a moment when we had to decide who would get the smallest room. Instead of flipping a coin, I volunteered to take the smallest room because I wanted the humblest setting I could possibly have.

I didn't have a meal plan, I slept in a glorified closet, and I worked three jobs at a time while going to school. In fact, throughout my entire college experience, I had a total of eight different jobs. Many of them were seasonal, temporary, or contract jobs that did not last. Due to my status as a full-time student, it was difficult to find something steady. However, even with all of that, I struggled to pay my bills. My rent was dirt cheap, yet I couldn't pull it off. There were weeks when all I could afford for food were rice, beans, a loaf of bread, and honey. I'm not joking. Two pieces of toast with honey was my daily diet sometimes. I was counting the cost per calorie of everything I bought, and I found that those items gave me the most calories for the least amount of money. Nothing will humble you like grocery shopping for the week with less than ten dollars. (If you think this sounds crazy, that's because it is. But it was the humbling experience I needed.)

Some of you reading this book may have had more humbling childhoods than I did. You may read this book and come across anecdotes that reveal my privilege, and you might scoff at it because you've faced much harder times throughout your life. If that applies to you, I want you to understand that adversity can be a good thing, if you choose to make it that way. It can be advantageous in the long run because building strength through hardship requires resistance. If this is true for you, then you are already steps ahead of where I was, and you're destined to become greater than I ever will be.

If you are on the opposite end of the spectrum, if you grew up even more privileged than me, please consider stripping yourself away from all of those sources of privilege, where possible, and experience going to bed hungry. They say hungry dogs run faster. I don't know if that is true, but I do know this: going to bed hungry made me appreciate everything my parents had done for me. It made me realize more than ever before that I had never earned anything in my life. The fire that that experience lit beneath me burned me to the core and propelled me to adopt a mindset to turn my challenges into resilience and to chase success—and, more importantly, significance—like a starving, rabid dog.

I realized that people all over the world are forced to live like this while I had taken everything for granted. More shamefully, I had taken for granted everyone who had provided me with everything I had. I realized that my grandparents had come to this country with the purpose of giving their children a better life—and their children did the same for us, my siblings and me. I shortly realized that there was nothing more I could provide to my kids, that my parents had beaten the game. I realized I would never be able to claim being self-made, but I could do something else: I could use the privileges and opportunities my parents had afforded me to build better lives for others. I could give back in a way my family never could because they had been so focused on building something for their children. I could promote change to help others experience the happiness I've been blessed with. And the book you now hold in your hands is just one of the ways I'm doing that.

I attest with absolute certainty that failing college was the best thing to have ever happened to me. It was the humbling smack in the face I needed and deserved. It was my first experience with real accountability. You may have heard the cliché phrase, "Karma's a bitch," but it's not true. That is only true if you fear accountability and avoid it. I've learned to appreciate that my actions have consequences, and it is my responsibility to manage my actions to produce the consequences I want. I've also learned that accountability is the foundation of love. Any relationship that lacks accountability is a relationship built on comfort and convenience, one that won't last when times get tough. That is why the relationship you have with yourself must be one built on a foundation of accountability. You deserve to have people in your life who keep their promises.

But that starts with you keeping the promises you make to yourself.

But, as the great Les Brown once said, "it's not over until I win." By looking at life this way, you can never truly "fail," as long as you keep playing the game. It really is that simple. As an athlete, when I was growing up, I lost many close games at the buzzer, knowing that if there had been just a few more seconds left, my team would have won. It is a truly crushing feeling, and any athlete or competitor of any type reading this will understand exactly what I am talking about.

What I realized as an adult is that there is no game clock in life. Whatever your goals are, the game is not over until you quit or you achieve your goals. Your losses are only real when you quit. If you have a dream job, and you interview for it and don't get it, you have two options: you can quit on that journey, or you can realize that the position will open again eventually and then commit to working to grow into the version of yourself that will achieve that goal and win. We race against a clock in our head, and when we imagine the clock striking zero, we give up.

But you don't have to live your life according to some imagined scoreboard. You can try a thousand times to do something before you get it right—and the beautiful part about life is that there is no scoreboard that says the score is one to a thousand. The result is the same. The goal is achieved. You are only competing against the version of yourself in your mind, which is commonly known as your ego. Get a healthy grasp of control over your ego and realize that there is no such thing as failing. There is only learning and quitting. If you learn and continue to try, you have not failed. If you learn and quit at the same time, you are wasting your knowledge by choosing not to apply it. You've experienced the pain to earn the knowledge, so *use it*!

Reframing Your Mind

My favorite neuroscience class in college was called Neuropsychopharmacology. (Well, it was called Drugs in the Brain, but that doesn't sound as cool.) There is a lot we have learned about the brain through experimentation with drugs, and one of those things is this: your brain processes emotional and physical pain in the same way (Roberts 2020). When people who have been experiencing emotional pain were given pain medication, they reported experiencing relief from their emotional pain. Your brain cannot tell the difference between emotional and physical pain. So, the pain you cause yourself with negative thoughts and self-doubt, your body experiences it the same way it experiences any physical pain.

Pain is your body's mechanism to draw attention to a problem; it is your body's way of telling you to change your behavior to avoid damage. So, if you have thoughts that are causing you pain, what is your natural response to the source of those problems? Avoidance. That is why the things that you are insecure about are the things you are quick to avoid. Avoidance behavior is a natural response to pain. Pain creates fear, and fear inspires avoidance.

That is why positively reframing your mind and your challenges is the key to overcoming your insecurities. It's not some hippie nonsense. It is a scientifically supported conclusion. Believe in yourself. Speak positively about yourself and create a sensitivity in your mind toward things that reinforce your positive beliefs about yourself.

Negativity Bias

The reason that this advice is so hard to actualize is because research shows that the human brain is significantly more sensitive to negative stimuli than positive stimuli. Going back to evolutionary psychology, this makes sense. It was important for their survival that our ancestors were quicker to identify—and have stronger reactions to—threats in their environment than rewards.

Unfortunately, this negativity bias shows up in our present-day lives very early on. In fact, the University of Iowa conducted a study and found that the average two-year-old child hears 432 negative statements per day and only 32 positive statements each day. With such a prevalence of negativity bias, it's up to you to reframe your mind and turn the tables on how you think.

Therefore, I practice writing affirmations daily. Your friends might laugh and make fun of you when you start writing affirmations, but it is a powerful practice. However, just saying positive things about yourself doesn't generate change. You must train your brain to believe those affirmations by practicing and by accumulating overwhelming amounts of evidence. Eventually, your brain will begin to grow more efficient at identifying evidence that confirms those beliefs; this is often referred to as confirmation bias. While confirmation bias can be a dangerous concept in research, it is often something that our brains use against us to form a negative perception of ourselves. When we make mistakes, those experiences reinforce our insecurities. Our mistakes act as evidence that we shouldn't have believed we deserved more in the first place, and that kind of thinking causes us to resort to our avoidance behaviors. To break that cycle, you must train your brain to become more sensitive to positive evidence that you are learning and growing in the direction in which you want to grow.

Here is an example: One of my insecurities is that I am an unorganized mess of a person. I tend to have a scattered brain and scattered thoughts. I am a creative, out-of-the-box thinker, and sometimes it is difficult for me to concentrate on putting every little thing in the right place. If you look at my office desk, you will see that I have papers scattered everywhere. Nothing is perfectly straight, as it ought to be. I am not very neat. However, if you look at the inbox for my email, you will notice that I have folders for everything. Everything has a place. For some reason (one I cannot explain), my brain prioritizes organization in certain places and not in others.

That does not mean I am unorganized. In fact, I am more than capable of being organized. I just value organization in certain areas of my life and not in others. It does not hurt my feelings if I walk into a room and things aren't perfectly organized. However, if I make a mistake that I think a more organized person would not have made, I start to look around the room and I see every misplaced item around me as a reminder of that mistake and a piece of evidence confirming my insecurity that I am an unorganized mess. It is almost as if my self-esteem is blind to all of the times and places where I am organized. Organization only pops into my head as a priority when I see evidence that I lack it. This is the negativity bias at play. We ignore or minimize examples of us doing something well, but we exaggerate our own flaws.

Part of reframing your mind is also allowing yourself the flexibility to change your course throughout your college experience. With new data comes new decisions. For example, it is OK to change your major. In fact, it is much better to make that switch than to continue to do something that will bring you no value in the long term. For anyone who disagrees, let me paint you a picture. I know hundreds of people—literally hundreds of people—who feel trapped in their careers. They are doing something they hate, but it is all they are "qualified" to do. Now they have a few options. In option A, they can leave that field and essentially start from the bottom elsewhere. However, that often means sacrificing their salary and taking a huge pay cut. In terms of life satisfaction, that may be a wise decision. But the problem is, if you have kids and you're already living paycheck to paycheck (as many people do), that is no longer an option for you. You are stuck working in a job you don't enjoy, for money that barely sustains your lifestyle, and suddenly you are trapped with no end in sight. Does that sound like a nightmare to you? Because it sounds like one to me. And it is the unfortunate reality for many. I want to help everyone avoid that position as much as I can.

OK, so what is option B? They can go back to school. There's nothing wrong with that at all. Some companies even offer tuition reimbursement programs. If they can take advantage of that, great! The thing is, if it takes them two or four years to complete that program, they are still stuck for that period. And tuition reimbursement programs often come with stipulations that they'd have to stay at the company for a certain period or else they'll have to pay that tuition money back. Which means they're going to be stuck even longer. And once they finally receive their degree, they must wait until a position opens at their current company related to that degree for them to move into. Again, stuck. And if their company doesn't offer tuition reimbursement, the cons are obvious. They are forced to take out more student loans or invest more money, and they'll have to use time that they could have used the first time they were in school if they had just switched their major.

The truth is, it takes strength and humility to realize that you made the wrong decision and then change your mind. You should always look back in time and know you could have made a better decision, because that is a sign of growth and progress. Be grateful for your mistakes, because they are what taught you the lessons that have made you who you are. But if you can't look back in time and acknowledge that you've made those mistakes in the first place, especially with years of new data, then you didn't learn the lessons you needed to in order to grow. And do you know what happens to those lessons? They are repeated until they are learned. The uncomfortable truth is that those lessons tend to be taught harder and harder until they are learned.

The challenge is to understand when to change your mind and when not to. Being stubborn has allowed me to be resilient. As you may have noticed from reading my story, resilience is an important part of my brand and of who I am. So how do you decide when to be resilient (maybe even mildly stubborn) and when to consider data from outside sources to help you decide?

My rule of thumb is that I am the only one who will own the outcome of my decision, and therefore, my perspective for my decision-making will always own 51 percent of the weight, at minimum. In other words, I don't ask ten people for their opinion and then vote on it. Your life is not a democracy. There have been situations where everyone in my life who loves me has told me that what I was doing wasn't the smartest decision, and I made it anyway, not because I don't respect those people, but because I trusted my instincts and didn't see those people as being more knowledgeable in that particular subject area. I also refrain from considering the opinions of people whose position I would not trade for my own. If you are contemplating a career decision, find someone whose career you would want yours to model, and then discuss it with them. Asking your friends who are in the same place as you could help you approach it differently, but the solutions they offer won't be backed by results.

I change my mind when presented with evidence that is supported by real results, from someone who has been through it and has achieved the results I am looking for. If you are a first-generation college student, you may find yourself receiving advice from family members who don't understand the college experience. Of course, you love and respect them, but are they in the position to give you advice? Or are they just as lost as you are and are trying their best? The goal is to find someone who has been there, done that, and can provide guidance from that lens. I hope I can serve as that person for you, if you don't have anyone else. This highlights the importance of surrounding yourself with the right people and asking them the right questions when you need guidance. However, it is not just the right people you need to surround yourself with… It is also the right environment.

Your Environment and Your Brain

There is another lesson from psychopharmacology research that is important for all young adults to consider: your environment impacts your physiology. For example, when you walk into your room after class, and you see your couch, your body will produce physiological responses to prepare you to rest, convincing you that you are tired and need to sleep, even when you don't need it. Your body has been designed, through the evolutionary process of natural selection, to adapt to your surroundings. It is powerful—your body identifies resources around you and prepares you to leverage those resources while they are available. The same is true for food. Have you ever found yourself bored, wandering around the house, and looking in the refrigerator, even though you aren't hungry? If you look at human history, developments like the refrigerator and the couch are relatively new. For most of human history, we have not had the ability to store food at safe temperatures and reheat it. Comfortable and safe places to sleep weren't in abundance, either. We did not have access to these luxuries in the way we do currently. So, when your body sees the cue of food or a comfortable place to rest, it naturally gravitates toward it because, from an evolutionary perspective, your body is unsure of when it will come across either one again.

This is another example of how the human brain can sometimes be counterproductive now that we live in an environment where our resources are in abundance. (Such as when your body is telling you to take a nap on the couch when you're not actually tired and you have homework due.)

The Myth of the Poor College Student

Speaking of having access to an abundance of resources… One of the ways college students set themselves up for failure is by repeating the myth of the poor college student. I work with student organizations all over the country as I help colleges and universities coach these organizations in how to operate more efficiently and maximize their impact in their communities. And when I talk to students about doing more for their communities, one of the common pushbacks I hear is: "How am I supposed to do that? I am just a poor college kid."

This sentiment frustrates me. Yes, many students struggle financially during college. I openly shared my story about struggling financially to highlight this. However, many of the students who view themselves as "just a poor college kid" live in dorms, with an unlimited meal plan and access to beautiful facilities like state-of-the-art gyms. Think for a moment about how much all of that would cost if it were in an apartment complex. If you are one of these students, please recognize that you are practically living in a utopia that exists nowhere else. Your first "adult" experience is setting wildly unrealistic expectations while you are simultaneously repeating the narrative that you are currently "poor" because you don't have money in your bank account.

Yet, you have access to an unbelievable number of resources, including a vast amount of social capital that you can leverage to meet experts in various fields. There are so many resources available to you; there are no excuses. You are not "just a poor college kid." Sure, you are busy, and you may not have a lot of money, but you have abundance in ways so many others could not even imagine. Take advantage of those resources instead of focusing on what you don't have.

Don't fall into the trap of perpetuating limiting beliefs about your situation. You are surrounded by more capital and resources than most of the world. There is most likely a student government budget, grants, etc. that you can dip into to fund projects that can not only generate widespread change but can also help you develop the life skills that can't be learned in a classroom setting or an entry-level job. One resource you won't be able to find on a college campus is time. Unfortunately, time isn't for sale. They say time is money, but the inverse is not true. Money can buy convenience and save you time, but you will never be able to buy a twenty-fifth hour in a day or an eighth day in a week. Be sure to use it wisely.

Principle One: Use Your Time Wisely

Once you realize the importance of having the right mindset and practicing it consistently enough to make it a part of your character, it will become your biggest key to success. I have developed two simple principles for an efficient and effective approach to academics that will help you throughout your college career. Following these two principles will shape who you are and will ultimately mold your destiny of success. While these principles apply to many aspects of life, they completely embody the college experience, especially during the transition from high school to your freshman year.

The first principle states: *One hour of preparation can save you two hours of work.*

If you're a procrastinator, this principle will change your life. College will make you think that twenty-four hours simply aren't enough to complete your to-do list and still have fun in the process. But I've realized that this simply is not true. There is plenty of time, if you use your time wisely and take advantage of every hour.

I used to pull all-nighters, cramming as much information into my head as I possibly could, studying the same topic for ten hours straight...and I failed miserably. We all have the same twenty-four hours in a day. College just teaches you a tough lesson about the relationship between supply and demand. You can't buy more time, so the supply never changes. However, once the demand for your time increases, so must the value of your time. You must make better use of your time by becoming more efficient with all your habits. This also means you must be more efficient with how you decompress mentally and emotionally. (We will talk in detail about self-care and stress management later in the book, so don't worry!)

College will most likely be your first time living completely on your own, free from the influences of other people such as your parents or other mentors. During this transition, you will experience stress in a way you're not used to. Remember, your environment is a strong dictator of your behavior, and as a result, this drastically new environment will bring out a different version of yourself that you may not have seen before.

After a couple of years of trial and error (and I mean *lots* of error), I had an epiphany. If I spread my ten hours of studying over a few weeks while I was learning the material, I would be able to retain more information. I didn't need to spend more time studying; I needed to prepare a plan that would enable me to use my time more wisely by studying more effectively. Psychological studies show that sleep is *crucial* for memory consolidation. This means that studying without sleep is almost pointless, because sleep plays an important role in your brain's ability to code, store, and retrieve memories. In fact, the amount of sleep you get before and after being exposed to the material is more important than the amount of time you spend studying the material. Yes, I said it: sleep is more important than time spent when it comes to studying. Therefore, compromising sleep to study is counterproductive.

So, what does this mean? If you start reading about and researching a topic the day before going to class, you will increase the amount of sleep you've had between learning about the subject and being tested on it, which will help you succeed. You'll also maximize the benefits of class time by doing so because, by studying the material prior to class, you will be hearing it for the second time in class, from a different voice, described in a different way. This will help you consolidate the information more effectively. The truth is, you really don't remember much of what is said in class. However, if the information is familiar to you (because you've already read about it before class), you are more likely to remember it. So, by doing that one hour of preparation, you will be saving yourself hours of work later. You'll realize this when you are trying to learn the information on the night before the test because you didn't understand the material when it was said in class. It will be like a foreign language to you the first time you're exposed to it—trust me.

You'll find that, in college, you are a professional in training. You are learning about a field in which you will later become an expert. Inherently, you will be learning an entirely new language that you'll use later among professionals in your field. And the earlier you expose yourself to that language, the quicker you will absorb the concepts. Essentially, doing your work early will save you *so much* time. You'll learn more during class and you'll be able to spend less time studying. The amount of work you have to do in a semester is already set. There is nothing you can do to decrease the workload. The only way to buy more time is to start the work as early as possible.

Principle Two: Making Sacrifices

The second principle states: *You must either make sacrifices in the process or sacrifice the final result.*

Over the next few years, you're going to realize that college is a phenomenal place that will provide you with an abundance of opportunities to make friends, get involved in a plethora of activities, and discover new attributes you never thought you had. While these aspects of college are equally important to your growth as an individual and as a future professional, you must choose how you'll spend your time on each type of activity. It is easy to say, "I will take a break from homework tonight to go out with my friends for a little bit," but moments like these are when this second principle is important. The moment when an opportunity to walk away from your work arises, remember that, if you choose to take the hard road now, it will pay off for you later.

In order to succeed, you must be willing and able to do things other people cannot or will not do. It's that simple. If you are willing to sacrifice going out one night to dedicate a few more hours to studying than most of your peers, you will reach places they cannot. You have to be willing to make those tough decisions. I promise you, the friends you want to keep forever are the ones who will understand. They may go out without you, but they will respect your decision to grind as hard as possible, and they'll support you in your endeavors. If you have a friend who doesn't respect your dedication, it's probably because they don't have that trait themselves. They will inevitably show their lack of dedication to your life as well. I don't want you to think that being successful in college means giving up your social life, because it doesn't. It just means you have to learn how to balance your activities well enough to make them all as healthy as they can possibly be.

To summarize it, do what others aren't willing to do, and learn to make sacrifices to balance your time. Get in the habit of doing the work as early as possible, because it will save you so much time and stress in the long run.

As a transformational educator, leader, and speaker, I have come to find that successful people value long-term fulfillment more than short-term entertainment. Make decisions based on the permanent impact on your life (and, if you're bold enough, for the generations that will follow), not based on the temporary feelings that manifest in the moment. You might find it difficult to prioritize long-term outcomes over short-term pleasures, and there is a scientific explanation for that. The truth is that the brain devotes more resources to pleasure-seeking systems than it does to rewards systems. In other words, your brain is inherently more interested in searching for something than finding it. The reward you experience from finding that thing will never match the pleasure you felt during the search, because that is how your brain is designed. This often leads us to perpetually seek new forms of stimulation. We scroll through our phones, check our apps for notifications, and seek new adventures in all forms. We want to meet new people instead of building deeper relationships with those whom we already know, we want to explore new places instead of appreciating the place we are in.

I'll never forget how excited I was when my wife and I bought our first house. It needed so much work, and we were so invested. Yet, months later when we were moved in and all of the work had been done, I found myself back on Zillow and looking for our next house. I was already looking to write my next chapter before I had the chance to enjoy the one I was currently experiencing. We are all guilty of this, in every phase of our life. It is important that you learn to recognize it early—especially during your college experience—and learn to control it.

This natural phenomenon is known as hedonic adaptation, or the hedonic treadmill. We set a goal, we chase it, we achieve it, and we celebrate. Then, what was once our goal becomes our new norm, and so we set a new goal, and the cycle continues. Do you remember that feedback loop I referenced in the beginning of this book? We are constantly stuck in that loop. That is why it is so important to learn how to enjoy and appreciate the process. You won't be happier when you get to the next stage. You won't be happier when you have more money. You won't be happier when you have that degree. Happiness is about gratitude and enjoying the process.

Success versus Significance

As you learn to sacrifice short-term gratification for long-term fulfillment, one important skill you'll need to develop is the ability to differentiate success from significance. Being able to make this important distinction will be key to helping you make those tough choices when it comes to deciding how to use your time wisely.

Tim Tebow, professional football player and popular speaker, explained the difference between success and significance beautifully. To illustrate, he showed a photo that has been considered one of the most influential pictures of our time, according to *Time* and the *New York Times*. The photo won the photographer a Pulitzer Prize, one of the greatest honors a photographer can receive. The image depicted a young girl who was starving, lying on the ground after trying to walk from her village to a feeding center. While she was on the ground, seemingly in pain, a vulture was waiting for her to become its next meal. The symbolism was so powerful.

The photographer had been advised not to touch anyone because illness was rampant in the community and he wouldn't have immunity in the way the local residents would. So he took the photo but did nothing to help the girl. He tried to shoo the vulture away, but it eventually came back, waiting patiently for what it assumed was inevitable. The photographer won the Pulitzer Prize, and four months later, he took his own life. We can hypothesize that maybe the photographer took his own life because he realized that a goal he had pursued so vigorously was not as rewarding as he had expected it to be, or he felt guilty for choosing to benefit from suffering without stepping in. Sure, there was the risk of disease, but there is little doubt that he could have accessed gloves and other PPE, if needed.

The point here is that success is fleeting. It is a quick high that you eventually come down from, just like we see in hedonic adaptation. But significance, on the other hand, doesn't have to come with an award. It is an everlasting impact. It is a purpose that keeps you continuously fulfilled. Significance is something that can't be taken from you and given to someone else. There will be a new Pulitzer Prize winner next year. There aren't many opportunities to make the kind of impact he had the chance to make on that girl's life. For me, my family is my significance. My grandparents had the job of coming to the US, my parents built the American dream for us, and my job is to live it and make their sacrifices worth it. I want our family story to be one that inspires generations to come.

This is why I encourage everyone to reflect as often as possible. Focus on what you are grateful for, spend as much time immersed in gratitude as possible. It is not about getting what you want, it is about learning to want what you already have. That is how you balance striving for success with enjoying the process of finding your significance.

This practice is also crucial for self-care. True happiness comes from prioritizing your internal peace above all else. Going to that party on Wednesday night to avoid the stress of doing your work won't bring you peace. It won't make that stress go away. But the pride you will feel for doing high-quality work, along with maintaining your sanity and your valuable friendships, *will* bring you peace—and long-term fulfillment.

True self-care is not salt baths and chocolate cake, it is making the choice to build a life you don't need to regularly escape from.

—Brianna Wiest

Be on guard against external influences that will tempt you to avoid making the necessary sacrifices. *Your* self belongs only to you; it does not belong to anyone else, and it is not defined by anyone else. Treat your self like your most prized possession, because that is exactly what it is. How do we treat other valuable possessions? We guard them. We have security systems and alarms in banks and jewelry stores. We have alarms on our houses and cars. We have fraud alerts on our accounts and credit cards. You must protect your focus on your ambitions with the same vigilance.

The alternative could end up costing you a lot more than you think. Just look at an example from my own mistakes: Imagine that I write you a check for $100,000 and I hand it to you. How excited would you be? How would that feel? Now imagine that you are on your way to the bank to deposit that check. On your way there, someone takes that $100,000 check out of your pocket and runs away. How angry or upset would you be? What would you want to do to that person?

Well, I have to look at that person in the mirror every day, because I am the one who robbed myself. Between losing my scholarship*, paying for an extra year of tuition, losing a year in earning potential, and missing out on a year when I couldn't invest in my 401(k), $100,000 is a conservative estimate of what my own mistake had cost me. Every single day, when we are doing things that are distracting us from what we need to do to learn and grow, we are doing exactly that. We are robbing our future selves of happiness and fulfillment, oftentimes for meaningless, short-term entertainment.

Going to that party to avoid the stress your work is causing you is only going to make that eye contact in the mirror the next morning more difficult. Make the sacrifice now, and get the work done so that you can look in the mirror and say, "I'm proud of you." And then go to that party with the extra time you've earned, not borrowed time from your future self. But make sure to still get the sleep you need to wake up and give tomorrow the energy it deserves.

* The college I went to has over a 70 percent acceptance rate and practically offered everyone a scholarship. The tuition was advertised as $50,000 per year, and then the school offered a ton of scholarship money as a marketing tactic to encourage enrollment. (And it worked; it was the only school that offered me a scholarship, so my parents were very excited for me to go.)

Step 2: Be Organized

College life offers a level of freedom you may have never experience before. And with that new freedom also comes new responsibilities, both in the classroom and out of the classroom. While responsibility can sometimes feel scary or overwhelming, with the right tools in your pocket, you can make the most of it and create transformational opportunities to create greater happiness in every aspect of your life. In this chapter, we'll look at some tools to help you get organized, which will make taking care of your new responsibilities infinitely easier!

Your college years will reveal what you do with a little bit of freedom, and ultimately, life after college will reveal whether you can handle all of the freedom life has to offer. The freedom of adulting is worth the responsibility, if you do it right. It's up to you to leverage your freedom and use it to live a life worth living. If you are free and unhappy, there is no one else to blame but yourself. It is up to you to ultimately define what happiness is for yourself and create that on your own.

Misconceptions about Happiness

- Happiness is not the absence of problems, it's the trust you have in yourself and your ability to deal with your problems.

- Feeling sad after making a decision doesn't always mean it was the wrong decision; it could just mean it was a tough choice. You are going to have to make tough choices, which will immediately be followed by negative emotions.

- Happiness does not rely on the approval of others. It can include moments of loneliness, but learning to enjoy your own company is an essential part of the journey. You will disappoint people who you believe to be your friends but who don't care about you in the way you need to care about yourself. If you disappoint friends by prioritizing yourself, that means they value the entertainment you provide them more than they value your well-being. That is not a true friendship but a trans action where you provide entertainment for free.

- You're not stressed because you're doing too much; you're stressed because you're not doing enough of what fulfills you.

- There will come plenty of moments in your life—and particularly in your college journey—that will make you question, *why does this keep happening to me?* The lessons you continue to struggle with will repeat themselves until you learn from them.

Step 1 illustrated the basic framework to establish the right mindset. Now, in Step 2, you'll learn how to develop your organizational road map for each semester, and each day, to turn that mindset into action! With your attitude and mind in the right place, you're ready to take on this challenge, and I want to show you how to be completely on top of your game at all times.

I'm going to show you two tools that work very well in conjunction with each other. You can use these tools however you prefer, in order to remain in control of your day and your time.

Agenda

The first tool is an agenda. I know this isn't anything groundbreaking, but having an agenda is crucial to maintaining a thorough record of what you need to do and when you need to do it. I personally prefer to use a printed agenda or planner. Widener University had a bookstore on campus that sold planners, which also included a calendar listing events that were happening around campus. I'm sure most universities have something similar.

I want to tell you how to take an agenda a step beyond the basic daily to-do list and use it to plan your entire semester before classes even start. If you're already in college, I'm sure you've heard this before, and if you haven't started classes yet, get ready to hear this quote a million times: *it's all in the syllabus.*

Well, as annoying as it is sometimes, it's true. The syllabus is a blueprint for what to expect in each class, and aligning your agenda with your syllabi will create a foolproof plan that you can follow throughout the semester. (I also completely understand that some professors make their syllabus intentionally ambiguous, and I will also provide you with insights on how to handle those cases.)

First, everything that is written on the syllabus calendar should be noted in your agenda, not just the exam dates. This includes quizzes, homework assignments, and everything else, down to which chapter you should read from the book each night. Why is this so important? Well, as we already discussed in the previous chapter, you should read a chapter *before* it is discussed in class, to help your brain better retain the information. So, by outlining each task in your agenda, you can keep up with what is going on amid all the chaos.

Adding all of your classwork tasks into your agenda also helps you see a big-picture view of your workload. For example, you will find that you will have some weeks when you will have an exam, a paper, a quiz, and a homework assignment all due in every single class on the same day. (Don't ask me how that happens, but it does.) By creating your agenda early in the semester, you can anticipate those troublesome weeks and plan accordingly. Or, if you know you have two or more big exams on the same day, you can start studying for them earlier than usual to avoid getting overwhelmed. You won't be able to prepare for these types of conflicts if you wait until the last minute to start studying.

You will also be able to observe trends. For example, maybe Wednesday is your busiest day of the week. If so, you can adapt by making that your rest day in your workout schedule. This is where that first principle from Step 1 arises once again: one hour of preparation saves you two hours of work—and an abundance of stress.

You can also write notes to yourself like "Create practice test" (see Step 3) a week or more prior to an exam so you know it's coming up without turning the page. This allows you to focus on each week, and particularly each day, rather than worrying about the future, because you know the warning signs are already in place.

Finally, for the professors who tend to create an ambiguous syllabus that lacks detail, go to their office hours within the first week of class—and bring your agenda—and ask them to help you sketch out the plan for the semester. They may not have all the answers you want, but you'll at least get some additional guidance beyond what was provided in the syllabus, and your professor (or their assistant) will respect you for making the effort, and that can go far. Developing relationships with your professors as a result of your effort will allow them to start helping you in ways they may not help other students, simply because you are trying harder. (We'll cover more on this topic in Step 5.)

Organizing Your Goals

Another huge benefit of being organized is that it can help you turn your large goals into bite-size daily baby steps. For example, while I was writing this book, I was also working a day job, hosting a podcast, booking paid speaking gigs, and building a leadership consulting company. Initially, each of these goals felt so huge and daunting that they became stress-inducing.

So, what do you do when you have great ambitions? You focus on taking one step at a time. Focus on what you can accomplish in a day, set daily goals, and sleep soundly at night knowing you're making incremental progress toward accomplishing your goals and you are one day closer—and 1 percent better—than you were the day before.

Instead of focusing on those large goals, I broke them down into daily steps. I printed out a weekly schedule and pinned it on the wall over my desk. One day a week was completely dedicated to the podcast. I would search for future guests, edit prerecorded episodes, schedule the publishing of edited episodes, etc. Another day was solely dedicated to the leadership consulting work. I would write articles, cold-call potential clients, meet with prospects, reach out to past clients to see how they were doing and to check if they had any unmet needs, draft and submit proposals, etc. Another day was dedicated to public speaking. I would record videos and post them on social media, schedule future posts, fill out calls for speakers, reach out to agencies that represented speakers, and create a pipeline of deadlines for future speaking engagements to apply for.

I knew that if I did these little things each and every week, eventually I would meet these big goals. I didn't have to build Rome in a day; instead, I focused on laying one brick at a time, and I trusted that, one day, Rome would be built. You must learn to do the same in college. Stressing about all of the work you have to do won't get the work done. Take each day one step at a time, maximize your time to the best of your ability, build strong habits and systems to manage them, and trust that the results will come. If you notice that the results aren't there, it is time to adjust and recalibrate.

There is a phenomenal TEDx Talk called "How to Achieve Your Most Ambitious Goals," by Stephen Duneier, that I encourage you to watch. He highlights this perfectly and shares real-life examples of how he applied these principles to his own life.

Google Calendar

The second tool is Google Calendar. Many people already utilize this awesome resource, but I want to tell you how you can use it to operate like a well-oiled machine.

When you have your class schedules set up, go on your computer and enter all of your class times into your calendar with notes, including their locations. This way, you won't have to worry about getting lost during the first couple of weeks of classes. You can then download the Google Calendar app on your phone, sync your calendar, and follow the notes that pop up throughout the day, without even having to think about it.

Once you have all of your classes in your calendar, you can add your meetings, work schedule, and workout schedule, and you can even determine when you are going to eat each meal each day. (Trust me, it can be easy to forget to eat when you have several classes and other responsibilities to juggle.) Essentially, you'll add every place you need to be onto your Google Calendar so you'll never miss a class, meeting, work shift, workout, or meal.

Notice that I've included tasks that are not related to academics; this is because getting great grades requires a sense of balance. Take care of yourself. Once all of those tasks are out of the way, you can decide when to study, hang out with friends, and take part in other important activities based on the gaps in your schedule. These gaps represent your opportunities to take out your agenda, see what needs to be done, and get to work on knocking out your to-do list.

I even added my bedtime to my calendar. I would get a notification about thirty minutes before bedtime to let me know that it was time to start getting ready. I would wrap up my final tasks for the day and prepare my mind and body to rest. I used Google Calendar to automate my life and operate on autopilot. I reduced the amount of cognitive resources needed to decide what to do. It had already been decided a long time ago, and now was my time to execute.

See what I did there? I showed you how to use the tools *together*. You'll use Google Calendar to tell you where to be, and then you'll use your agenda to tell you what to do when you get there. As long as it isn't something as obvious as breathing, taking notes, or picking things up and putting them down, it should be in your agenda.

To make this relationship between your agenda and your Google Calendar even more effective, I have one last step for you: *add "Outline tomorrow in agenda" on your Google Calendar*. About thirty minutes before your general bedtime each night, you should look over what you have to do tomorrow so that you can be prepared. You should also repeat this process in the morning by briefly looking over your agenda before starting your day. This will allow you to be on task, and it will prevent you from overlooking goals you've set for yourself. Having these tools at your disposal, and using them in this way, will allow you to get into a rhythm of putting attitude into action and developing good habits.

Make the Most of Your Time

Time is arguably the most precious resource in life, and yet, because it's also finite, you can't afford to waste it. As you learn to integrate your newfound organizational skills into your college life—and beyond—you'll start to see how being organized will help you make the most of your time.

The thing about time is, it gets shorter as you get older. This is a mathematical fact. Every day is slightly shorter than the last one, or at least, that is how your brain processes it. Time is relative to perception, so one year of your life will always be perceived as one divided by your age. When you are ten years old, one year is 10 percent of your life. When you are fifty years old, one year is 2 percent of your life. Each year, that percentage will get smaller, and therefore, every year will go by faster. This means that, each year, your mind will tell you that it is shorter than the last. So make the most use of your time while you have the most of it!

Do yourself a favor and volunteer to spend time with elderly people in a retirement home. Ask them, if they could go back and do anything differently, what they would change in their life. Their answer will almost never be that they wish they had worked more or made more money. Most likely, their answer is going to be that they wish they had spent more time with their friends and family. But, in order to do that in your own life, you need to use your organizational skills to protect your time and offer you the flexibility to use your time in the way you want to. Doing things right early in your life during your college years—and continuing those practices in your career and throughout your life—will offer you the opportunity to do that.

If you start doing research on personal finance and financial literacy early in life you will learn about a concept called compound interest. When you invest money, it accumulates interest, and over time, your interest will accumulate more interest, and this process continues to generate wealth. The earlier you invest, the more your money compounds. The same is true with building strong habits. If you start now by creating and those habits, and you continue to build on them throughout your life, you will find that you will not only achieve success (as you choose to define it) earlier, you will also experience more of it.

> Compound interest is the eighth wonder of the world. He who understands it, earns it; he who doesn't, pays it.
> —Albert Einstein

Leverage compound interest in each aspect of your life, and watch how fast it grows. It does not just apply to money; it applies to everything. Take fitness, for example: the better shape you are in, the farther you can run. The farther you can run, the more calories you can burn. The more calories you are capable of burning, the more nutrients your body can absorb without adding weight. The more nutrients your body can consume, the more it can use. The more resources your body can recruit, the farther you can run. And the cycle continues.

The same is true with studying and learning. The more effective you are at implementing the strategies we're discussing about studying, the faster you can learn. The faster you can learn, the more time you will have for doing other activities. The more time you have, the more you can accomplish, which will also lead to more learning opportunities. I realized that becoming the fastest learner I could would be the best skill set I could develop in life.

Build habits that revolve around the learning process, be organized, and be intentional, and watch how fast your life changes for the better.

Step 3: Develop Good Habits for School

With your eyes set on the prize, and your organizational road map created, it's time to do the hard part: developing strong habits. This also means not just letting old habits die, but aggressively dismantling them. Trust me, it's going to be painful. I know, because I had to go through an immense transformation to go from failing to becoming a dean's list student. But I promise it'll be worth it.

Being at the top of the class in academics is like being at the top of any field; it requires working harder and smarter. You have to study your craft. Yes, I am telling you to study the art of studying…and I know that doesn't make much sense right now, which is why I have done the "studying" for you. During my time as a psychology student, I tried to understand how to best utilize the powerful brains we have as humans. I have come across some very interesting discoveries, and while I promise not to bore you with the details of methods and statistical analyses, you'll see that psychology is at the heart of every habit I'm about to share with you in this chapter.

Reading Aloud

Remember the first principle from Step 1? *One hour of preparation can save you two hours of work.* When discussing the importance of preparation, I explained that, by reading the textbook the night before class, you will already be familiar with the topic by the time you're in class and listening to the lecture. This helps you remember the information better because of the role sleep plays in memory consolidation, and it also helps you absorb the information better. Well, one way to take this habit a step further is by reading the material *aloud* to yourself before each class.

Hearing information you've heard before boosts your memory retention because of your recognition of the information. When you hear new information—for example, when you're reading the text aloud to yourself, the night before class—your brain codes it and stores it for later retrieval. Then, the next day, when you hear that information again in class, it reactivates the portion of your brain responsible for the storage of that information. You are effectively strengthening the neural connections in that portion of your brain, and therefore, you're improving your memory of the information. This is why I highly encourage reading your textbook and notes aloud. You read the words, speak the words, and hear your own voice saying the words, absorbing the information in three ways.

Associations

We all have an incredible capacity to make associations. Everyone remembers their math teacher using acronyms to teach them the order of operations, right? Associating information with a pattern of some sort will help you remember it. One powerful way to utilize our ability to recognize associations is by incorporating things you already know into the new information. If you like basketball, for example, associate as much information as possible with basketball.

This may not always be feasible, but try to create associations between your interests and your class topics whenever you can. This process will become easier as you progress through college and hear more content from more classes because you'll also find yourself creating associations between topics from other classes. When you manipulate information to create associations with the material, your memory on the topic will become drastically stronger.

Take a Break

Not only do we have a predisposition to remember associations, but we also have a tendency to remember the beginning and the end of what we hear. It is a natural tendency for us. This is known as the serial position effect. If you are sitting in a lecture for an hour, you are more likely to remember things that were said at the beginning of the lecture and things that are being said toward the end. The middle of the lecture will have blended together. This is because that information wasn't associated with moments of transition or significance. There is also research that shows that spatial awareness plays a key role in memory. There is a book called *Moonwalking with Einstein* by Joshua Foer in which the author recounts his experience of becoming a memory champion. He started investigating how people could remember an incredible amount of information while others (like me) forget the name of someone who literally just introduced themselves. He found that the former group of people tend to use tricks to help them remember, including using their memory of spaces they know well (like their house or their office) and tying newly learned information to objects in those spaces.

So how can you use this to your advantage? During your study hours, get in the habit of frequently taking short breaks. You should not be studying for more than thirty minutes at a time before taking a break. The longer you study without a break, the more information you are going to forget from that session. Create as many beginnings and ends as possible to help you remember the information better.

During your break, think about what you learned in that short session; this will help you consolidate the information while you're also relaxing. For example, eat a small snack, or do something else like you're your laundry, while you think about what you were studying. Any small task that gets you away from the textbook or laptop and isn't mentally draining will suffice. Do something that involves moving around a little bit, as associating new information with new spaces will help. If you are working on your fitness at the same time, go on a short walk around the block while you think about the new information you learned. Don't stress about it while you walk, make it nearly mindless and pleasant. If you have a three-hour study session, and you take six walks around the block, you'll increase your steps, destress, and increase your chances to retain more information. That sounds like a win-win to me.

Question and Answer

I will now share a habit that will help you take notes more effectively, which will help you prepare for your exams and quizzes. The best way to take notes while you're in a lecture is not by rushing and writing aimlessly, as many students do. Instead, the goal is to come up with as many questions as possible, and then answer them.

While you're reading the textbook the night before class, you should turn every bold heading and word into a question. Also write down the questions in the review section at the end of the chapter. Then, while you're in class, write down every question the teacher asks. Your notes from class should be in the form of questions, followed by material relevant to those questions.

You're not going to see information on the test; you're going to see *questions*. This is why the best way to prepare for a test is by preparing for the questions, not by memorizing information. Besides, you will notice that many professors post their presentations or notes online after class, so there's no need to scribble furiously and try to catch every word from the lecture.

If you come prepared to class, you'll have an idea of how to answer the questions presented in class because you've already studied the material the night before. If you don't, you didn't prepare properly for class. Don't wait for the test to study; think of every class session as a test that should be studied for.

Speaking of preparing questions, the best way to study for an exam is by creating a practice test with every question from your notes and an answer sheet for it. You should create the practice test a week prior to the exam so that you can bring it with you to class. Then, you can approach your professor about any struggles you may be having when answering certain questions, rather than struggling on the exam. You can also take class time to ask the professor to answer one of the questions on your practice test as an example. If you can master the skill of building practice tests, and ace those practice tests, you will inevitably ace the professor's test.

Study Your Professor

I'm going to point out something extremely obvious but also paramount to your success: the teacher is the person who creates your tests and determines your grade. Consequently, you should spend part of your class time focusing on studying the professor. When you are in class, mark your notes with symbols associated with your professor's behavioral cues. For example, if the professor walks around frequently, create a symbol in your notes to indicate that this is occurring when certain questions arise. Other cues could include what they do with their hands or when they add emphasis to certain words or ideas.

Also pay attention to the clock. Write down the time intermittently, maybe every ten minutes, throughout your notes. Since you are writing down questions, cues, and times, you can pick up on trends in the professor's behavior. I know I'm teaching you to think like a psychologist, but trust me when I say that it works. You may notice a professor only tests you on questions that were asked at the end of class because they spend the beginning of the class introducing the topic and they wait until the end to get into the important information. On the other hand, a professor may provide important information in the beginning of class and then ramble off track toward the end.

You may also notice that a professor asks exam questions that can be found at the ends of the chapters in the textbook, or they may not reference the textbook at all. You may notice a professor likes to pace a lot during class, but the moment they stop moving is when they ask exam questions. When you finish taking your test, look back in your notes right away, circle questions that appeared on the test, and look for patterns.

You will realize that professors have tendencies, and this will help you predict what will be on the test. This will save you an abundance of time because you will know exactly what to study, because you've already studied your professor.

This is why class time is so important and why you should never miss a class. You will not only miss information, examples, and potential exam questions, but you will also miss cues in your professor's behavior. You may miss hints for what to study or what isn't worth studying. Treat class time as though it were precious, because that is exactly what it is. College can cost up to one thousand dollars per credit, making many classes worth upward of three thousand dollars in total. Missing a single class is wasting an expensive opportunity to learn and develop your professional future.

Getting in the Flow

I had the pleasure of interviewing Milena Regos, the founder and chief rebel officer of Unhustle, on my podcast, *The Pursuit of Self-Actualization*. She talked about the importance of work-life balance and how we, in fact, have it backward. Even when we talk about work-life balance, we still put work first. Milena built a marketing company that was generating tens of millions of dollars in revenue, but ultimately, she found herself feeling completely burned-out and unfulfilled. She noticed that other executives were experiencing the same thing. She realized that she had built a life that modeled success as others defined it. She decided to change that, and she started a company teaching high performers how to "unhustle" and build a life intentionally. When I interviewed her, she shared some profound insights that I have built into every aspect of my life. It was not something I understood during college, but I wish I had.

She taught me about flow states. Chances are, you have experienced flow states at some point in your life, without even realizing it. Have you ever been so focused on an activity, task, or conversation that suddenly you looked up and noticed that hours had passed? That experience is known as a flow state. They make focusing on something feel effortless. Research shows that people can be up to five times as efficient when operating in a flow state. This is because flow states occur while the brain is leveraging gamma brain waves. Essentially, the brain operates by sending electrical signals; however, these signals occur at different frequencies. Gamma brain waves travel faster and move throughout the entire brain in ways that other brain waves do not. This means that gamma waves serve as a key to achieving optimal brain function.

There are scientists who study flow states and share how to create them in your life. Milena shares that information with busy executives so they can accomplish more in less time and then use that time saved to spend more time with their families and doing things that are rewarding. I want to help you apply those concepts to your college experience.

Remember when we talked about using Google Calendar to automate your life? That is one of many strategies that can help you reduce the amount of cognitive resources required to make decisions. The moment you stop what you are doing to think about what to do next, you are leaving your flow state. When you are worrying about the time and how much time you have before you need to move on to your next task, you are leaving your flow state. Instead, this practice allows you to fully immerse yourself in a task and trust that your phone will interrupt you when it needs to. You will then see that notification on your phone, start packing up your things, and be on the move to your next class or task.

The only thing that could distract you from your work would be your phone telling you to go to your next thing, nothing else. When I did this in my own routine, I went into my phone settings and turned off the notifications for every other app. I no longer received Facebook or Instagram notifications. I no longer received text notifications. The only thing that my phone would do would be to update me about my next move. I eliminated all distractions.

Music also plays a key role in flow states. For example, I would listen to instrumental music that gave me energy and focus. By eliminating the vocals, I was able to concentrate without parts of my brain focusing on rehearsing the lyrics. The music selection will vary for each person, so listen to instrumentals for the style of music you enjoy, but not songs you know. If you listen to an instrumental for a song you know every word to, you will find yourself reciting those words without even trying to. That is taking away from the task.

I also noticed that I was in flow immediately after a workout. So, what did I do? I started working out first thing in the morning and doing my most challenging work immediately after my workout. I studied my most challenging subjects and did my hardest homework assignments; essentially, I built my life and my schedule around when I would be at my peak performance. I structured my schedule to put me in the position to do my best work when it mattered the most. Imagine going to your first class and having already completed the three hardest tasks of the day: waking up, working out, and completing the work or studying for your hardest subject. The rest of the day will be spent riding that high all the way through your tasks. Everything else will feel easier and in the flow.

Don't go through college with the goal of getting the work done and getting good grades. Focus on building the self-awareness to design a life that is spent in flow as often as possible; the rest will take care of itself.

Practice, Practice, Practice

Developing these habits during your college years will pay dividends for your future in big ways. Treat school like your opportunity to practice being a professional before your livelihood depends on it. Failing a test is stressful, but when that test becomes a project that gets you fired because you couldn't perform, it will be significantly worse.

Nail your habits down and learn how to be disciplined about working them into your routine. This is where you transform and grow; this is where your future begins. You can choose to skate by and do the bare minimum, or you can take control of your future and achieve great things that inspire you and those who will come after you. Your college years are when you can develop those habits that will create your solid foundation.

If you approach your education in this way, I guarantee you will make the dean's list every single semester. Remember to maintain a positive attitude, because *you* control the outcome. Believe in yourself and your dreams, because I promise you, people will call you crazy for shooting for the stars. Be willing to do what others won't, because then you will be able to live a life that others can't. Be organized and diligent in your habits, because that's how you will control your future. And finally, no matter what you do, strive to be the best version of yourself that you can be. Now that you are a college student, you should strive to be the best in every classroom. In order to do that, you need to constantly be looking to learn more about your field, as well as yourself.

Step 4: Develop Good Habits for Life

Now that you've started to implement impactful habits into your approaches to classes and studying, it's time to look at how to develop good habits in other areas of your life. Whether you want to transform your physical fitness, nutrition, sleep, or any other goals you might have outside of the classroom, the habits discussed in this chapter will help you make meaningful progress every day as you keep moving forward.

The Neuroscience of Environmental Factors

Did you know that your environment is a major driving force of your behaviors and habits? It's true! Neuroscience research shows that your brain prepares you for the behavior it expects to perform when you enter a new environment. For example, have you ever noticed that when you're home, and you're walking around doing things in the kitchen, you suddenly find yourself looking in the fridge, even though you really aren't hungry? You just look because you're there. That's because you are naturally wired to search for food when you enter the kitchen, regardless of whether you're hungry. The same goes for relaxing. You may have all the energy in the world, but when you walk into your living room and lay your eyes on the couch, your body starts to feel tired, and your energy begins to fade.

Scientists first noticed this trend in people who struggled with addiction. When people who have developed substance abuse habits see stimuli related to the drug, they experience symptoms the drug counters. For example, someone who is addicted to painkillers will begin to feel pain when they see a person consume those drugs because their brain is responding to their environment and triggers pain signals that would then be alleviated by the drug they're addicted to. Your brain is doing the same thing to you all the time, in response to the stimuli surrounding you.

Manipulate Your Surroundings to Change Your Routine

How can you make this law of neuroscience work to your advantage? By making changes to your environment so you're surrounded by stimuli that prompt you to follow good habits!

For example, falling asleep and waking up early have always been challenges for me. Here is how I have resolved both issues to build healthier sleep habits by manipulating my surroundings. In order to make falling asleep easier, I started by building a nighttime ritual. I stopped watching TV, looking at my computer, or looking at my phone about an hour before I planned on going to sleep. I turned my room into a place where I only did two things: go to sleep and wake up to get ready for the day. I never relaxed in my room, and I never did any work in my room. I did work in the library, at the computer lab, in the cafeteria, or anywhere else on campus where I could spend long periods of time focusing.

I made my room a temple reserved only for sleep. Now, when my body enters my bedroom at night, it knows what I am there for, and it prepares for sleep. I started getting into this rhythm, and it helped tremendously. The lack of stimuli in my bedroom environment helped because it set clear expectations for what my body was supposed to be preparing for. Over time, falling asleep became extremely easy.

Now, the next part: waking up. I realized that the farther I placed my alarm (which is my phone) from my bed, the more likely I was to get up instead of hitting the snooze button. So I started charging my phone on the opposite side of the room, which meant that I'd have to walk to it in the morning if I wanted to hit snooze. While that helped, I still had some issues consistently doing this. Over time, I began grabbing my phone, hitting the snooze button, and then walking back to my bed. I was seeing progress, but it was not quite a full transformation. I needed to make another change in my environment to really create a lasting change.

I have a two-story home, and my bedroom is on the second floor. So I began charging my phone by the bedroom door, I moved my bed to a different wall so it would be even farther from the door and the phone, I purchased an alarm clock, and then I added that second alarm at the bottom of the stairs. Now, when my alarm goes off, I have to walk toward the door to turn off the first alarm, and then I have to walk down the stairs to turn off the next one. At that point, I am closer to my cup of coffee than I am to my bed. I have to work harder to go back to sleep than I do to start my day. You can even go as far as getting one of those coffee machines that you can set on a timer to have it start brewing your coffee at the same time when your alarm goes off. Now you are waking up, and you are immediately introduced to a stimulus that you will be attracted to—the smell of freshly brewed coffee—and that will help keep you awake. This is how you begin to manipulate your environment to improve your opportunities for success. Make it easier to do what you need to do than it is to maintain the habit you currently have.

You might be saying to yourself, *Well, I don't live in a two-story house, I live in a dorm room with a roommate…what do I do now?* This is when it is so important to be transparent with the people in your life and try to get on the same page. In my freshman year of college, I had a roommate who was in ROTC. My life would have been a million times better if I had just woken up with him and went running or went to the gym when he woke up for ROTC. (And his life probably would have been better if he hadn't had to worry about waking up his lazy roommate while doing what he needed to do to succeed.) If you're in a situation like this, encourage your roommate to go on this journey with you. Coordinate with your roommate, get on the same morning schedule, set goals that are in alignment with each other, and work together as a team. Now, if they aren't on board with it, that is their problem. You can't let someone else get in the way of what you are trying to do. Do everything you can to be fair and considerate, but don't compromise your own good habits to appease them. If you can't get your roommate on board, it might be helpful to find someone else in your dorm who shares your values and can hold you accountable, and go on the journey with them.

As I began getting better and better at waking up early, I had to build on that momentum. I began setting up other cues in my environment to make sure I was doing what I needed to do once I woke up. Waking up at four o'clock would mean nothing if I was just going to scroll on my phone and watch Tik-Tok videos. So, to encourage me to work out in the mornings, I started sleeping in my gym clothes. I realized that the time I was spending in the morning to pick out my gym clothes was more time spent near my bed, which also meant more temptation to lie down and scroll or go back to sleep. By waking up, going downstairs to turn off my alarm, and already being in my gym clothes, I had no reason to go back upstairs. My coffee was already brewing, and all I had to do was put on my socks (which I would leave in my gym shoes by the front door the night before) and shoes and get moving. I would even leave my supplements out on the counter next to the coffee machine so that I would take my supplements, drink my coffee, and be ready to go for the day.

I also started leaving my journal on the dining room table before I went to bed. Why? Because when I was done with my workout, I would shower, get dressed for the day, come back downstairs, and eat breakfast. Leaving my journal on the table—where I would eat—increased the odds that I would journal and reflect after breakfast. What did journaling do? It helped me focus on my goals, and it inspired me to write. Suddenly, I had all of these healthy habits and I was knocking pages out of writing this very book.

Essentially, I turned my house into a trail of breadcrumbs that would lead me from one healthy habit to the next. This is going to look different for each person and in each situation, but I want to challenge you to start thinking the same way. How can you shift elements in your environment? How can you switch up your routine in a way that makes each healthy step seamlessly follow the last? The more friction you create between two things, the harder you will have to work to make them fit together. Your goal is to create as little friction in your life and in your habits as possible.

Just as a car can only go so far on a tank of gas, the same is true about your brain. You only have room to make so many decisions and deal with so many stressors in a day. Your goal is to reduce the number of decisions you need to make, because each one costs you energy and essential cognitive resources. Make the process of making the right decision as easy and as simple as possible. Do not force your mind to fight other forces; make it a passive process by manipulating your surroundings.

Now, my routine before I go to bed is to set up all of these breadcrumbs for myself. This gives me an opportunity to put away all of the distractions that had once prevented me from going to sleep in the first place, and it encourages me to keep the habits that will help my morning self thrive. It subconsciously teaches my mind that it is about to be bedtime, and it prompts my body to start preparing for sleep, which makes falling asleep easier. And while my brain is doing that, I am also using the last bit of my cognitive resources for the day to save my morning self from using them when they are at their most precious, when I can make decisions that will compound throughout the day to build a successful day.

The Importance of Journaling

As you work on manipulating your environment and developing good habits, journaling can be an essential tool for pushing you over the finish line toward reaching your goals. By journaling about your behaviors and habits each day, you'll gain valuable insights into what's working and where you can improve.

Treat yourself like a science experiment. Try various routines, and then journal about how you feel at certain times of the day:

- What habits help make you most productive?

- What routines keep you running like a well-oiled machine into the evening?

- What tweaks in your environment help you get the best sleep?

- What actions make you feel sharp, motivated, and confident?

- What activities charge you up, and what activities drain you?

- How can you move your schedule around so that you can save the draining activities for last and use them to help you fall asleep quickly?

Journal in the morning, in the middle of the day, and at night until you find the best routine for you. Then, cut the journaling down to morning and night, and focus on journaling for productivity and creativity purposes, rather than for routine and self-discovery purposes.

In the beginning stages of writing this book, my time was split in so many directions, and journaling helped me gain clarity on where I could make changes to achieve my goal of finishing this book. At that time, in addition to writing, I was also completing my master's degree, teaching, building a business, and buying my first home. (Oh, and that home was a fixer-upper that my wife and I were working on ourselves.) During this time, I also made a career change to advance myself as a pioneer of education, technology, and human development. I had been laid off due to contract disputes between my employer and a customer, and then I found a new job and was laid off due to COVID-19. I had four jobs in less than two years, and I relied on that income to pay for the house, invest in my business, and pay for everything else. You can imagine I was making very little progress, at best, on my book during this time period. Journaling kept me sane in the darkest of times, and it also helped me learn about myself and my stages of productivity.

Due to all of the changes that were going on in my life at that time, I was looking for ways to establish some consistency. I wanted to create a series of routines that would help me perform at my highest level and keep doing so in a sustainable manner. I'd already started making the changes I discussed earlier, and they were effective. I was feeling extremely productive, I had more energy, I was getting in better shape, the list of pros could go on and on.

However, there was one consistency—which I found in my journal logs—that made me question if my routine was optimal. I noticed that I was so profoundly inspired by the process of writing this book, but I couldn't spend as much time writing as I wanted to because I was working during the day. I am one of the few blessed people who can say that I thoroughly *love* my work, but my routine was causing me to resent my job because it felt like it was taking me away from doing something I was inspired to do. But it wasn't my job's fault. (After all, I wouldn't be able to afford the bed I sleep on at night if it wasn't for my job. My job provides way more than it takes away.) I realized that I had to adjust my routine to wake up a few hours earlier so I could get my morning workout in, slow down the process of getting ready to enjoy it more, and then journal in my home office by 5:30 a.m. so I could spend the next two hours writing my book. That adjustment alone allowed me to finish this book, and it eliminated the resentment I was feeling toward my job (which, in turn, improved my overall job satisfaction), while also removing a distraction and increasing my productivity at work.

You may have noticed that I nonchalantly grazed over the fact that I started waking up a few hours earlier, like it was nothing. I can humbly admit that I did not snap my fingers and make this happen. It took trial and error, it took commitment, but it was one of the smallest sacrifices I've ever made that has yielded some of the greatest benefits. Not only did it help me finish this book, improve my productivity at work, and increase my satisfaction with my job; it also made me a better partner, friend, and family member. You see, before waking up earlier, I would come home from work feeling tired, and I'd make something quick for dinner and then relax for a bit before getting mad at myself for not working on my book. Dinner was just something I had to do, something that stood between me and this book. But at that time, I was already too exhausted to do it. So I either hated myself for not having the energy to do what it would take to finish this book (which also made me less enjoyable to be around), or I actually got up and locked myself in the office to finish it. Either way, I was missing quality time with the people I love. I noticed that, when I changed my routine and my habits, I was able to *be* home—not just physically being present, but mentally, emotionally, and spiritually being home. My mind wasn't locked away in my negative thoughts, and neither was my body locked away in the office. Dinner wasn't a chore to throw together really quickly; it was my last task of the day, the day I had spent building momentum by doing everything at a high level so that there was no reason to stop. I was investing more time in dinner and enjoying the process. As a result, I was eating better food, spending more time with my family, and being a more enjoyable presence in their lives. A small change in my habits helped me be happier, healthier, and more productive in every single phase of my life—and I only noticed this opportunity for improvement by reviewing my previous journal entries and searching for trends.

In addition to being a powerful tool for assessing your routines, getting in the habit of journaling can also help you transform any negative thoughts and detrimental self-talk into empowering, positive affirmations. David Goggins is a renowned athlete and author, and he is an amazing example of sheer determination and relentlessness. (He wrote a book called *Can't Hurt Me*, and I highly recommend it to everyone.) He was a guest on the web show called *Impact Theory* (which I also recommend), where he talked about how he went from being fat and lazy (his words, not mine) to being considered one of the most badass people on the planet. He talked about the importance of going to the "dark place" in your mind and listening.

That dark place is an echo chamber of thoughts that haunt you. It's where you store all the lies that other people have convinced you of about yourself and you then internalized. If you have never experienced anything like this dark place I am talking about, I want you to know that I hadn't either, prior to coming to college. Once you are on your own, things begin to rise to the surface that you didn't know existed inside of you. You will experience a lot of firsts as a college student, and that series of new experiences will reveal behaviors you may have never expected. You may one day look in the mirror and realize that you don't recognize yourself anymore. The person you see staring back at you can be a better version of yourself, someone your high school self would have looked up to, or it can be someone you are ashamed to be, someone you wish you had never become. This process I am going to walk you through will ensure it is the former and not the latter. You don't have to fail the way I did to experience the same growth.

When I was failing college, this was exactly what I did, and it was not by choice. Any negativity I had experienced in the past came rushing back in an overwhelming barrage of voices in my head that I thought were my own, because I was hearing them from my own conscience. But as I began journaling and writing what those voices were saying, I was able to step back and think about where they were coming from, and I realized that those voices were not my own words at all. They were the voices of my teachers, my father, my old friends, strangers, and anyone else who had doubted me. At first, I wanted to be angry at all those people, but then I realized something. Do you know how many other conversations I've had with those people? Do you know how many things they've said to me that *weren't* negative? It was *me* who was echoing those thoughts. It was *me* who had locked their words away in a vault where I could access them whenever I wanted to be self-loathing. It was *me* who was repeating those words repeatedly. And most importantly, in the end, it was *me* who proved them right.

You see, we already know that our thoughts become our actions, our actions become our habits, and our habits determine who we become. I had chosen to internalize those negative thoughts and become the failure they destined me to be. As I journaled during my darkest times, I found all of my insecurities, I found all of my vulnerabilities, and I found the version of myself that I had to be in order to keep them alive. I learned how that dark place in my mind had been constructed. But that didn't stop me from going there. It's like when you stumble upon a new place, but you don't know exactly where it is or how you got there; you just know the place exists and what it looks like. So, I had to figure out how to stop going there, how to shift my negative self-talk.

This highlights the importance of journaling for metacognition. Now that I had identified that dark place and understood its importance, I was able to start working on dismantling it. So, I started journaling every time I found myself feeling depressed or doubting myself. I started asking myself questions. *How did I get here? What train of thoughts led me down this path? What happened that sparked that train of thoughts?* As I started doing that, I realized things about myself, things I was sensitive to, triggers that would send me spiraling. As I learned about the various downward spirals that would lead me to my dark place, I was able to disrupt those thoughts and processes. If I recognized early enough that I was heading down that path, I could intervene and pull myself out.

Your negative self-talk is not *who you are*. You are not unorganized. You are not incapable. You are not irresponsible. You may have exhibited those behaviors, but they do not define you. Behaviors can change, but they can only change when you begin dissociating those behaviors with the fabric of who you are. They can only change when you believe you are powerful enough to change them. As David Goggins said, "you have to be your own hero." I was my own worst enemy. I was my own villain. I was projecting the pain I was inflicting on myself onto others, to avoid responsibility. But once I started owning the choice, I'd made to internalize those thoughts, I empowered myself to change the narrative.

So, I filled that echo chamber with new, empowering voices. I started journaling affirmations every day that contradicted the thoughts that used to haunt me. I wrote things like: *I am organized. I am capable. I am responsible.* And then I would write a list of small examples each and every day that proved those affirmations right. The craziest thing that started happening afterward was that I started to remember positive interactions and conversations I'd had in the past with the same people I used to think were the cause of my insecurities. I started being more aware of my small victories, which built momentum toward bigger and bigger victories. It was a small shift in my mindset that made a monumental difference in my life. Every time I made a responsible choice, even the smallest one, I would get a reminder in my brain, almost like a notification on my phone, a message from my subconscious that I was on the right track.

You already know why it's important to surround yourself with stimuli that remind you to do the right things, that keep you on track. Journaling about your dark place and writing your affirmations can be an important part of that positive stimuli. Your daily affirmations will remind you of your strengths and will drown out your insecurities. It is important to constantly remind yourself. As we know, the more often you think or experience something, the more you strengthen the neural pathways in your brain that are responsible for perceiving and performing those behaviors. Reminders are crucial. The more often you go to that dark place in your mind, the easier it will be for you to go there in the future. Each trip down that road seems to go quicker and quicker. The same thing applies to your affirmations of your greatness. The more often you do it, the more sensitive you will become to anything that reminds you of those affirmations. We are biologically designed this way. Understanding how your brain works will allow you to have better control over it and use it to your advantage rather than feeling trapped.

Another powerful habit I started incorporating into my journaling routine was signing my journal with my name, with a slight twist. I would write my name with my goals as my middle name. For example, I would sign it Dante 160TriathleteVP2022NYTBestSellingAuthor DiBattista. I know, it is crazy long, but the point is that I was constantly reminding myself of the version of me I wanted to create. I put my target weight (160), my athletic goal (triathlete), my career goal (VP by 2022), and my goal as an author (become a *New York Times* bestseller). I didn't just write my name; I wrote some things I wanted my name to mean and be associated with. I did that every day, along with my affirmations that countered the narratives in my mind that were preventing me from being that ideal version of myself.

All the positive behaviors that turned my life around stemmed from my habit of journaling. I reverse engineered the echo chamber and used it to my advantage. That is the power of metacognition. Think about your thoughts and create behaviors that rewire your perspective. You control the lens through which you see the world.

The results? They were even better than I had expected. I reached a director-level position at the age of twenty-six, was interviewing for VP positions at the age of twenty-seven and decided to instead completely leave the workforce to become my own boss by the age of twenty-eight. This book may never become a *New York Times* bestseller, and quite frankly, I don't care. I want it to change your life for the better. If it achieves that, then I hope you will choose to share it with someone else so that it may change their life, too. If it changes enough people's lives enough to be worthy of sharing, I believe it will become a bestseller. The label doesn't matter, it's about the impact.

Accept More Responsibility Than You're Ready for, Don't Avoid It

Another useful habit is to train yourself not to shy away from taking on responsibility, even if you feel you may not be ready for it. The version of myself at the beginning of this story—the one who failed out of school—would typically run away from responsibilities. I feared accountability, and I did the bare minimum to get by. That was not the version of myself that would become a self-employed, best-selling author and thought leader in my area of expertise. It required that I see responsibility as an opportunity, as a blessing. Think of every opportunity to do more for someone or something in your life, and pick one more thing to do for that person or organization. Watch how quickly you will become a leader in that organization and watch how quickly the people around you will become just as invested in your success as you are.

That mindset shift doesn't have to start with goals as grand as building a business or changing the world. My puppy, Luna, was a gift, and at first, I was not ready for her at all. I could barely pay my bills, I was working multiple jobs, and I could barely take care of myself. My landlord at the time did not permit animals, so I had to worry about getting kicked out of the house where I was living. Accepting the responsibility of caring for Luna put me in a challenging situation that forced me to consider other options. My landlord allowed me to finish out the lease, but I could not extend the lease like I had planned so that I could stay there next year. I couldn't move back in with my parents because my father is allergic to dogs—and that would have kind of defeated the whole purpose of the journey I was on, anyway. The solution I came to was to move in with my grandma. That decision pushed me to spend priceless time with my grandma that I otherwise wouldn't have had.

I spent my last year of college helping to take care of her. My grandfather had passed away six years prior, and after that, my grandma started to really deteriorate mentally. She barely left the couch, including using the bathroom. I found myself cooking for her, helping change her, washing the pads she slept on, and cleaning up after her. Suddenly, because of this puppy, I was now caring for someone who, for most of my childhood, had cared for me. I wasn't fully aware of how bad her situation had become until I moved in with her. My mom had previously taken on the responsibility of taking care of my grandma, and Mom was always the person who would extend herself beyond her means to care for others while asking for nothing in return.

I moved in over the summer, but once school started for my final year, my grandma helped take care of Luna. She would let her out and feed her. Suddenly, she was getting off the couch and moving around. She started getting back into a bit of a routine. Her helping me with Luna gave her a purpose she had felt she'd lost. Unfortunately, it was too little too late.

My grandma ended up passing away about two weeks before I graduated college, during the finals week of my last semester. Luna was the reason I had spent the last year of my grandma's life with her. It became the most precious year of my life. During her final stay in the hospital, she was in a great deal of pain and was not mentally present when I'd visit her. She was crying and yelling for help, and it was my name she called. Even when I was in the room and was talking to her, she couldn't hear me but continued to call out my name for help. It was the most excruciating moment of my life. Yet, it made me realize that, for the past year, I had served as someone she could turn to for pain relief and purpose.

Embrace responsibility—run toward it, not away from it. So many of us are told by bitter old folks to enjoy being young and having no responsibilities while we can. Sure, being young and having no responsibilities to tie you down is fun. And yes, time is moving faster than you could even imagine. But the fact is, if you do a basic cost-benefit analysis, it's simply not worth it. Embrace responsibility as much and as early as you possibly can. This time period only lasts a few years, but you deal with the consequences of your irresponsibility for a lifetime—and what they don't teach you is that the costs of those mistakes compound over time. And conversely, your responsibilities will compound throughout your life to bring you more happiness and success.

Stress Management and Your Perception of Stress

There was a study on stress that consisted of a simple two-question survey of over thirty thousand adults across the US. They asked how much stress the participants experienced, and if they believed stress was bad for them. Then, they followed the public death records to see who among the surveyed population died, and if there was any correlation between their answers to the survey and their long-term health.

After following the participants of the study over the long term, they found that the *level of stress* did not determine how long someone lived or how healthy they were. In fact, it was that last question—*how they perceived stress*—that was the strongest indicator of their longevity. The people who saw stress as a good thing were the ones who lived longer. How can you see stress as a good thing? Well, stress can be a powerful tool. We evolved from the experience of stress because it shifts the mind and body into a different gear that we otherwise wouldn't have. Initially, it helped us survive because those of our ancestors who had stress were more driven to escape from predators or acted with more urgency to find food for their families. In this way, stress can be a good thing. You would not exist without it. Embrace it.

However, it is also taxing to the physical body. The stress hormone is called cortisol. Long-term exposure to high levels of cortisol can lead to heart issues, among many other health issues. The goal is to learn how to manage your cortisol levels and have a healthy relationship with stress. I interviewed Andrew Oakes, the founder of Stress Relief Headquarters, and during our conversation, he made me realize that we often reward our stress, causing us to experience more of it. Think about it: what do most people do when they are stressed? They do things they enjoy, or they turn to their vices. We get stressed, and we drink a beer or glass of wine. We reward ourselves for experiencing stress. That is not building a healthy relationship with stress.

Instead, the goal is to build a life around experiencing stress while doing things that challenge and inspire you and building healthy stress-relief activities into your daily habits. This includes prioritizing your physical well-being, eating healthy foods, spending time outside, and having healthy relationships with people you love.

You Have So Much More Time Than You Think

Another element to stress is understanding that life is not a race, and there is no reason to rush through it. We stress ourselves out over timelines and the belief that we should have accomplished more by now. During this journey that college will take you on, you may find yourself feeling overwhelmed and feeling like there just aren't enough hours in each day. Let's look at how you can shift your perspective on time. While it may not feel like it, you have a lot more time than you think.

As I've mentioned throughout this book, I am lucky enough to interview successful entrepreneurs, athletes, authors, and influencers through my platform, and one of the most powerful lessons I've learned from them is how much time we truly have in our adult lives. It is hard to conceptualize when you are in high school or college but look at my own story as an example. I graduated college at twenty-three years old, and at the time of the publication of this book, I am now twenty-nine. That means I am six years into my adulthood. The average life expectancy for a male in the US is currently around seventy-nine years old. That means I am only six years into my fifty-six years of postcollege adulthood. Let's fast forward to when I'm forty; I will still only be seventeen years into my fifty-six-year journey (if I am lucky enough to reach the average). So, when I am forty years old, I will only be finishing the first quarter. Every athlete knows that if you are worried about the scoreboard at the end of the first quarter, you have already lost the game. Instead, focus on enjoying each day and making the most of it. There is no game clock you are competing against, there is no one else running this racetrack with you. I have interviewed entrepreneurs who started their businesses in their fifties. I have interviewed people who sold their businesses in their forties to become educators because that is what they love. Changing your major and graduating a year later is not the catastrophe it may feel like in the moment. Even if you fail out and come back to graduate in your forties, you can still say you did it.

Your stress is often self-imposed. Don't create more stress for yourself by rushing the timeline; instead, live a rewarding life built around the intention of becoming someone you are proud to be, surrounded by people who love you for being that person, while making the world a better place by solving problems that you are uniquely capable of solving.

The Human versus the Machine

One thing you might encounter as you go through this journey of improving your habits is that you might find you're focusing so much on optimizing your performance that you start to lose touch with who you are trying to become as a person. This is something many successful people I have interviewed have talked about experiencing. It is an internal battle. You work so hard to reach your goals, and one day you are finally there, and you start thinking about the next goal, the next milestone, the next A on your transcript, the next award you want to receive, the next list you want to be included on. Essentially, you become so goal-driven that you lose touch with what is important. If you find yourself feeling more like a self-improvement machine and less like a happy human, remember this:

The machine is a means to build the person you dream of becoming. You are not just a sack of emotions, and you are not just a machine. By finding balance and learning to build a healthy relationship between being a high-performing individual and someone who is in touch with their sense of purpose in this world, you can create a Terminator-like badass who makes the world a better place, who makes the people around them better for knowing you, and who enjoys the journey as much as possible along the way. It is possible to have both, but it requires strict intention. It doesn't require being strict about everything you do (unlike what most people will tell you), but it requires being strict about your intentions and the alignment between them and your behaviors.

When it comes to the college experience, you probably hear people telling you not to go to parties. The truth is, I'm glad I went. I'm glad I had fun and built friendships with people. Striving to be the best version of yourself does not mean sacrificing everything that brings you joy or being a robot that only does things that make you money. It means finding healthy ways to celebrate. I go to parties, but I don't drink heavily. There are periods of my life when I won't drink at all. I will still go to the bar with my friends, and I'll just drink water and will go home at a reasonable time. If you are on a diet and are cutting out cake, that does not mean you have to skip birthday parties. Just make sure you bring food that aligns with your diet and skip the cake. Or anticipate how many calories of cake you plan on eating, and include that in your meal plan for the day. You are allowed to relax and have fun—you are not a machine. Be intentional about your goals, and don't stray so far away that you can't redirect yourself and go back. You can have your cake and eat it too. You can be successful and enjoy life.

Learning Is a Lifelong Journey

As you begin to put these new habits into your routine, remember to strive for progress, not perfection. You are always going to be improving and learning. And a great way to embed this into your perspective is to see learning as a lifelong journey.

Many students bring to college the idea that they are there to learn everything they need to learn, get a degree, and be able to get a job—and that is the end of their learning journey. I have years of experience in HR, and I can tell you that, not only is that not true, but if you express that mindset in an interview, you are almost guaranteed not to get the job.

College is your opportunity to learn a specialized set of information and show you can apply it and are willing to do the work to learn to become an expert. But it will take decades of continuing this process on your own, in your own time, *after college*. If you are under the impression that getting your degree means you're an expert in your field and you can stop learning, I have news for you: it doesn't.

If you want to advance yourself in your career—and in your life, in general—you will be constantly learning and seeking new opportunities to grow your skill set. That might mean learning about a work project, going home and researching methods to execute on that project, and preparing for the next day so you don't make a mistake and lose the opportunity. Even beyond your career, your life should be a perpetual learning project. Continuously seek to learn how you can be a better friend, family member, partner, community servant, etc. All of the roles you play in your life should be roles that challenge you to grow, and it is up to you to make that happen.

Understand There Is Always an Alternate Route

If you find yourself stressed out over the path you are on and you're thinking maybe you can't finish it, just know that there is always an alternative. For example, I found Teach for America (TFA) as an alternate route toward getting a teaching certificate. I then used my relationships with TFA to get into Johns Hopkins University, a school I wouldn't have gotten into using a traditional approach. I used my background in psychology and IT to begin consulting tech companies as a learning and development subject matter expert. Suddenly, at twenty-six years old, I became the director of training for a company. That is not the route most people would have taken to get into that role, but that doesn't matter. Your journey does not have to follow a traditional path. Don't panic if things aren't going your way; there is always an alternate route.

Step 5: Build Connections

My last piece of advice is to meet as many people as possible throughout your college years, learn from all of them, build new relationships, and appreciate all the long-lasting ones. College is a place to make connections and utilize the ones you already have, such as friends, family members, professors, counselors, classmates, etc., so take advantage of it!

As you go about your day-to-day activities, you'll have opportunities to meet so many people who can help shape who you are, give you direction, and help you reach your goals. I could write a whole chapter on the importance of building connections... So, I did. And, in this chapter, you'll find guidance for creating valuable relationships inside the classroom, on campus, and off campus.

Stand Out from the Crowd

You might remember from Step 1 that we all have an inherent, evolutionary drive to be a part of a group. This goes way back to our hunter-gatherer ancestors. And it's true—finding people you can connect with and fit in with is an important part of building connections in college. (We'll dive into that later in this chapter.) But don't make the mistake of trying so hard to fit in that you simply fade into the background. This is especially important to keep in mind in the classroom, where standing out from the crowd can reap huge rewards. I'd like to share a few personal stories to use as examples.

My first example comes from when I was in a class called careers in psychology. In this class, I had a professor named Dr. Simons, and her job was to help get people into practicum positions. (A practicum is essentially an internship that counts for credits toward graduation. If your school offers these programs, I highly recommend you take advantage of them. The class I was taking happened to be a prerequisite to the practicum program at my school, but I'm sure other schools approach it differently or maybe have a different name for this type of program.) While I was in this class, I was putting in the effort to write every paper as well as I possibly could. Each paper involved doing research on the field of neuroscience, which I planned on entering at the time. When Dr. Simons read about my passion for research, she couldn't ignore it because it flowed through every one of my papers. It was evident and powerful.

One day, I received an email about an opportunity to be a research assistant. The email stated that Dr. Simons had referred me and said I would be a perfect fit for the position. I was not actively seeking positions; we didn't even get far enough into the course for me to learn about all of the options for positions to start applying for. However, because I was putting in the extra effort and was writing my papers with passion and purpose, my professor created an opportunity, and an offer was extended to me.

A university is an elaborate network with people who have connections all over campus and in a multitude of fields. Professors are people, too. They all go to work every day and spend time with their colleagues, just like in any other profession. They develop relationships with their coworkers, just like anyone else, and they talk to each other. Use this to your advantage by standing out and being the topic of conversation; you never know what offers may be extended to you. If you stand out and grab a professor's attention, they will think of you when other professors inform them of their searches for students. They could be searching for an assistant or a student to take to a conference of professionals in your desired field; the possibilities are endless!

My second example is when my psychology adviser, Dr. Ayers, saw how much I enjoyed talking about topics related to neuroscience. He recognized how knowledgeable I was on the subject because of the abundance of studying I was doing outside of class. Most of my studying was out of pure interest, not because it was required, and it showed. He knew I had received a job as a research assistant, and that I would be looking for more opportunities to gain more research experience once that study was complete. My résumé had plenty of leadership in student-run organizations and entry-level job experience but none that particularly related to my field of interest. He knew about my situation, and he offered to help.

One day, I walked into Dr. Ayers' office for a routine advising meeting, and it turned out to be far from routine. He informed me of an opportunity that would be perfect for me. Oklahoma State University was offering to pay ten students from around the country to travel there and participate in a summer research program revolving around current topics in neuroscience. The program required that you read about the ten professors participating and pick the three you would be most interested in working one-on-one with based on their laboratory studies. When I picked the three professors, I was most interested in working with, Dr. Ayers contacted them personally and advocated for me. He explained that nothing on paper could define me because my story was unique. The amount of growth I had experienced during college trumped the growth of many of my peers as a result of my failures and the work I was putting in to overcome them. He advocated for my work ethic, character, and maturity. You'll notice that these are aspects of my personality that he could have only understood by communicating with me outside of class.

Dr. Ayers had heard about this program through an email newsletter he'd received from a group of neuroscientists from many schools across the country. They use this email list and newsletter to communicate with each other about opportunities exactly like the one I just mentioned. He could have thought about many other students with higher GPAs, but he chose me because of how I stood out, not just as a student but as a person. (In case you're wondering… No, I was not accepted into the program. But the point of this story is that I would have never discovered the opportunity on my own. Not every door will be open to you, but you can't try to walk through a door unless you know where it is.)

Chances are that your professor didn't graduate from your school. This means they have connections at colleges elsewhere in the country. It's also likely that they keep in contact with the people they graduated with, who went somewhere else in the country to work as well. Do you see where I'm going with this? The network of professors on your campus extends all over the country, and in many cases, throughout the world! I know from experience. If you have dreams to live and work somewhere different upon graduation, college is your chance to make important connections to get you there.

My final example is Dr. Schwartz, the director of the Oskin Leadership Institute at Widener University, which holds workshops, courses, and events designed to bring students and faculty together to grow as leaders. Before I met Dr. Schwartz, he had been formally named the faculty adviser of my fraternity, Alpha Tau Omega. I was familiar with his reputation on campus, but I hadn't had the chance to meet him. However, the day I met him became one of the greatest blessings of my life.

One day, I was walking back from class when I saw Dr. Schwartz leaving the Oskin Leadership Institute. In that moment, I knew I had two choices: I could continue walking, or I could stop where our paths would eventually cross, wait for him, and introduce myself. This wouldn't be a story worth telling if I'd decided to continue walking, so clearly, I chose the latter. I introduced myself and asked him what he was up to, just creating small talk. As it turned out, he was on his way to his car, which was in the parking lot that was in the direction I was heading anyway. I walked him to his car, said it was nice to meet him, and walked home.

The next day, I received an email from Dr. Schwartz requesting a meeting with me. He didn't provide any background information; he only said that he wanted to have a meeting. I was slightly nervous because I had no way to prepare for this meeting, and in my past, I had found that ambiguous meetings usually meant I was in trouble. But I had a feeling this might be something different.

When I walked into his office, Dr. Schwartz greeted me pleasantly and explained the purpose of our meeting. He was a part of a group that had created the first ever Collegiate Leadership Competition, and he wanted me to participate. Solely based on our conversation, he felt I would be a fit simply because of the energy I'd emitted. He didn't know me as an outstanding student, a hard-working young man, or an intellectually gifted individual. He just felt something in his gut during our conversation, and he thought I was worth believing in. Dr. Schwartz had also inquired about me to one of my fraternity brothers who had spoken highly of me. As a result, I was the final student he selected to participate in the competition. Just before Dr. Schwartz had walked out of his office on that evening when we first met, he'd received news that one of the people he had initially selected had to back out. I was in the right place at the right time. I wonder how often this happens—and how many people choose to keep walking, unknowingly missing life-changing opportunities.

The point of this story is that if you create positive energy and take time out of your day to get to know people, you never know what can happen. Dr. Schwartz became my mentor throughout the Collegiate Leadership Competition, and he continues to be my mentor today. I would never have built such a strong relationship with him if I hadn't been involved in that competition, which I would never have been invited to if I hadn't stopped to spark up a conversation.

The connections you create with your professors can have ripple effects that will open up exciting new opportunities. Soon after my practices had begun for the Collegiate Leadership Competition, I received another email. It was from my dear friend from Brazil, Ismael, who had joined Alpha Tau Omega during my time as the new member education program coordinator. He was developing an urban leadership project to implement in high schools throughout his hometown. He wanted to inspire the youth of Brazil and challenge them to be leaders, to stand for something and get involved in social issues that would make a difference in their cities and their country. After Ismael explained this to me, he asked me to help him come up with activities and workshops for these future leaders. He'd selected me because he had seen my success in making changes within our fraternity. I felt somewhat daunted by Ismael's request because I still had so much growing to do myself. I knew I would need guidance. Luckily, I was able to turn to Dr. Schwartz, who I knew would be the perfect adviser for such a project. We worked on it together over the summer. (Yes, I said it, over the summer. I was meeting with one of my college professors over the summer to work on a community service project.) That project became one of the biggest deciding factors for the Office of Student Life Awards Ceremony at my college, and I was awarded the Most Outstanding Community Servant Award. I wouldn't have been able to pull it off without Dr. Schwartz's contributions.

Coincidentally, the day I received that award was the day I also announced that I would be traveling to South Carolina to serve in the AmeriCorps Teach for America program. And I learned about Teach for America because of an opportunity that had been provided by Dr. Schwartz. During my senior year, I was taking one of his courses. One day, I showed up early, and so I struck up a casual conversation with him. He asked if I had any plans yet for spring break, and I told him that my girlfriend (who is now my wife) and I had been working multiple jobs all year to save up for a trip to Greece. He was so excited for us, but he was also excited to share that Widener University has a partnership with a school in Athens, Greece, called the American Community School (ACS), where Greek students are taught an American curriculum in English by teachers who are certified in the United States to prepare them to attend universities in the US. In fact, Dr. Schwartz told me that, within a month or so, the president of the ACS would be visiting Widener University, along with other ACS staff members. Dr. Schwartz had dinner plans with one of those staff members, and he invited my girlfriend and I to come along. During that dinner, we shared with the staff member that we would be visiting Greece, and she invited us to come to the American Community School to talk to some of their students who were interested in attending Widener. We loved the idea, and during our time in Athens, we did exactly that. We were dazzled by our experience in Greece, and we thought about how cool it would be to live there. Out of curiosity, we asked what it would take to work at ACS, and they said we simply needed a teaching certificate. Neither of us were attending school to be teachers, so we started looking into alternate teaching certificate programs, which was how we learned about Teach for America.

While we never returned to Greece, we did fall in love with Teach for America and its mission. We were both accepted into the program, and when we asked to be placed together, they kindly respected our wishes. Teach for America has partnerships with many of the top universities in the country, which is also how I got into Johns Hopkins University for graduate school. With my GPA from undergrad, I had zero shot, but Teach for America's preferred admissions gave me the leg up I needed.

As if this story is not serendipitous enough, eight years earlier, I was visiting my brother, who was attending Towson University, near Baltimore, where Johns Hopkins is located. He was a freshman in college, and I was only a sophomore in high school. He took me out to a party, and it turned out that it was thrown by Johns Hopkins students. I told my older brother that Johns Hopkins was my dream school, and he said I would never get in. It took me eight years, failing out my first time around, and taking some alternate routes, but he was wrong. I did get in.

From the first day when I took a chance and introduced myself to Dr. Schwartz, he went out of his way to nurture the potential he saw in me. For example, soon after we first met, he offered to buy me any book I wanted. He explained that there was money set aside in the Oskin Leadership Institute's budget specifically for purchasing books for students to keep, with the intention of helping to facilitate a growth mindset. Now, if you didn't think I was crazy already, this story will surely tip the scales. My choice was a neuroscience textbook. Not one I needed for class, but a textbook I wanted because it was touted as the best textbook available at the time on the subject I was most passionate about. Upon hearing my book choice, Dr. Schwartz was apprehensive at first and asked if it would be OK to buy the used version since it was such an expensive textbook. (Honestly, I was shocked he was even willing to buy the used version!) He saw my passion for neuroscience and leadership, and he decided that he had an idea to get the return on his textbook investment.

He also offered me the opportunity to do an independent study with him. An independent study is essentially a course where you, as the student, write the syllabus on your own, according to certain standards and criteria set by the professor. Once they've accepted your syllabus, it is completely up to you to complete the research project. Your entire grade is based on the final paper and presentation at the end of the semester. In my case, I had weekly or biweekly meetings with Dr. Schwartz to go over my progress, and he would give me the opportunity to ask questions, although it was all very self-driven. Together, we decided that my research topic would be the psychobiology of initiative; in other words, the relationship between the brain and behavior as it relates to initiative. What part of the brain is responsible for initiative? Why do some people have it, and some don't? Can it be developed? If so, how so?

It became almost an undergraduate dissertation. It was an in-depth literature review where I pulled sources from nearly every subsection of psychological research and paired that with neuroscience research to connect the dots. I reviewed over fifty textbooks and articles on these topics, and I found some profound information. I made some connections that I was not able to find from other researchers. It seemed that one bit of information was missing to link all my research together. As it turned out, that piece of information was tucked away in that textbook I had asked him to purchase earlier. I did not cite anything else from that textbook for this study, only one tiny bit of information, but it was the perfect glue that brought everything together.

That research propelled my career and helped me realize that I can bring a unique perspective to leadership development by focusing on the relationship between biology, psychology, and leadership. That is exactly what I do for a living now, and I wouldn't have known it was a possibility had I not participated in this project. It was the perfect blend of the success I experienced as a transformational leader on campus, my passion for neuroscience and psychology, and my skill set.

So, to put it all into perspective, because I had set myself apart by introducing myself to Dr. Schwartz, I was able to create a connection that ultimately led to a whole host of new opportunities. He was the first person on campus—outside of fraternity/sorority life—to identify me as a leader, and then he gave me opportunities to show it. He bought me a textbook that I'd wanted for my own self-education but couldn't afford. He helped me make connections abroad and gave me a bit of inspiration to consider living elsewhere—something I had not thought about much prior. Then that connection led me to finding a program that matched all my interests and aspirations. It even opened the door to attending my dream school that I was told I would never get into. He further challenged me to prove that I could be a thought leader in the fields of psychology and leadership, and he gave me the platform to do it. This opened the door for me to become the leadership development expert and public speaker I am today. And to think, I could have unknowingly walked away from this man and everything he had to offer. College will try to make you feel like you must fit the mold. Don't fall for it. Standing out from the crowd, making an impression on others, and taking the time to make connections and build relationships is all worth it. One connection can change your life. Be sure to choose your connections wisely.

The Power of Your Network

When I went through the Oskin Leadership Certificate program, the final step was to create my own philosophy of leadership, and then create a workshop that would help other people live out that philosophy. The goal was to create my own vision for my leadership style, and then bring that vision to life. My philosophy was simple: *Perceive no limits.*

I believe the limits we see for ourselves are fundamentally flawed because we, as humans, can achieve anything when we utilize our networks and work together. I, as an individual, may not be able to achieve something. But if I can articulate my vision clearly, and in a compelling manner, to the right people in my network, then we, as a team, can get it done. Even if the vision is so grand that it will take centuries to complete, we have the power of writing, and the power of history books, that will tell our stories long beyond us to inspire the generations that follow to pick up where we left off.

That is why I chose to create a workshop for networking—not just the basic concepts of networking, but the application of creative and strategic thinking around networking to empower others to believe they can overcome the boundaries of possibility that they have set for themselves or have allowed others to set for them.

Get to Know Your Professors

Now that you've seen a few examples of how standing out to your professors can lead to great opportunities, I'd like to present you with a very simple challenge: develop a relationship with every single professor you have, and then watch where those relationships take you. A powerful network will be your greatest resource after leaving college, not your education. A piece of paper can only get you so far but knowing the right people in the right places can get you anywhere.

Here are a few tips to make this happen for yourself:

1. Immediately locate your academic support services office. Your campus may have a different title for it but find the office that's responsible for supporting students' academic success. They typically have resources to share, seminars for you to attend, and all kinds of information and support to offer. Attend everything you can, right from the beginning of your college experience. They have lots of insights to offer.

2. Become close with your faculty adviser. Do not avoid meetings with them or see them as a burden. They can truly enhance your college experience far beyond scheduling next semester's courses, if you allow them to.

3. Show up early to class and stay after class to talk to your professors. This will probably be harder if you're on a large campus with large class sizes. If this is the case for you, you will just have to work extra hard to make it happen. Some professors will show up right as class starts and will leave immediately after it is done, but keep trying, no matter what. You also may come to realize that the professor is not the one you are going to build this kind of relationship with, and that is OK.

4. Strive to create a personal/professional relationship with them. Not all of your professors will be open to talking to you about things out side of class, but that's alright—you won't know until you try. (Remember, talking to Dr. Schwartz about my spring break trip to Greece led

to me meeting students from ACS and researching alternate teaching certificate programs, which ultimately led me to Teach for America and opened the door for me to attend Johns Hopkins for graduate school.)

5. Stop to talk to your professors whenever you see them on campus. For example, at my school, some of the professors ate in the cafeteria, which presented a great chance to stop and say hi. Not every professor is going to be accessible but be sure to take advantage of the opportunity when you see one. You never know what meeting they just left or what conversation they had prior to you approaching them. They could be thinking about what student to extend a great opportunity to, and you walking up to them could put you in the front of their mind (just like what happened in my first encounter with Dr. Schwartz). Additionally, professors walk around campus and see thousands of their students, only to get a nonchalant wave or to be completely ignored. Be the student who stands out by saying hello.

Get Involved Outside of the Classroom

Get involved on campus. Whether it's joining a group, playing a sport, or running for a position in student government, there are so many incredible activities you can be a part of on your college campus that are happening outside of the walls of the classroom. It is crucial that you do not let these opportunities pass you by. These types of activities are great for networking and self-exploration.

For example, you may realize that you want to pursue a career related to the work you are doing in a group on campus. Maybe you never saw yourself as a money person before, but you became the treasurer of an organization and learned something new about yourself. If nothing else, you would learn the basics of money management in a way that a class couldn't teach you. You've probably heard successful entrepreneurs on social media talk about why you don't need college, because it doesn't help prepare you for business or the "real world." Well, that's not quite true—there are some aspects of college that can set you up for success in the professional world. And running an on-campus organization is one of them. I don't care what organization you choose—if it has a budget, an executive team, and members, and if it is doing something you enjoy or care about, join it. Watch how it is run, learn about the challenges and strategic decision-making. Become invested in that organization's growth and explore your strengths that can be used to help make that happen. When you find your strengths and apply them to help that organization grow, you'll find what you can be best at in the professional world.

For me, that was training and education. During my sophomore and junior years of college, my fraternity was on the brink of being shut down. After consistently getting in trouble for multiple semesters and not being allowed to recruit as a part of our sanctions, we were about to close simply because we were graduating all our members without bringing in any new members. We needed to undergo a drastic culture change to survive as an organization.

I decided that the way I would help us do that would be by reimagining what the new member onboarding (aka pledging) process would look like. I decided that our bonding events weren't going to include hazing activities— not only because they were getting us in trouble, but also because they weren't effective. Instead, I built a process around real team building. I challenged our new members to analyze what it meant to be a better version of themselves, and how being a brother meant holding each other accountable to fulfilling that mission together. I explained that our organization needed them to be bigger and better people if it was going to survive. I held résumé workshops, academic support workshops, leadership development training, and many other activities that were devoted to facilitating growth.

The result? Two years later, shortly after I graduated, the organization's executive board was composed entirely of people who had gone through my process, and we won a national award for the first time in our chapter's history. The leaders I helped develop became the leaders who turned our organization into an award-winning team. That was when I realized that I had a knack for facilitating transformational experiences. That was when I realized that teaching, leadership training, and transforming organizational cultures was my calling. There was no class I could have taken to show me this side of myself. There was no textbook on it. It was something I had to learn through experience on campus. (And now I am the one creating those classes and writing those textbooks.)

That is why it is essential for you to get involved on campus. Find out where your strengths are and how they can support an organization. That is where you will find your place in the professional world. Even if you're studying something technical, like engineering, but you love working with people and recruiting, you have found a powerful niche in the technical recruiting space. Or you can continue your path as an engineer, and when it is your turn to lead teams, you can be more hands-on in the recruitment process to help you build the most successful team in the company. This is something an engineering degree will not teach you.

Think of it this way: your major should be something you enjoy studying, something you enjoy learning about. Your participation in organizations outside of the classroom should help you identify what professional capacity or business unit you operate best in. Then, your career focus should be getting into the unit that maximizes your skills within an organization that specializes in the field you enjoy learning the most about, because you will spend the rest of your life learning about that, I assure you.

If you approach college this way, if you prioritize building a strong network of amazing people, and if you learn how your skills can help an organization excel, you will get way more than your tuition's worth from your college experience. Your experience won't just be educational, it will be transformational.

Transcendence and Helping Others

In an earlier chapter, I referenced the hierarchy of needs, and I told you that self-actualization is the highest level of human motivation. But since that research was first published, a new tier has been proposed for the top of the pyramid: transcendence. Once you reach the place in life where you are independent of the desire for esteem, and once you realize that validation from external sources is not the true meaning of success and happiness, it is your job to build a legacy by helping others. (You are currently holding the first building block of my own legacy.)

Once you learn how to become the best student of life, it is your responsibility to become a teacher. That transition is difficult, and it's much harder than the one you are experiencing currently. However, once you overcome this obstacle in your life, you will develop the strength to conquer that next chapter, as well. And I will be here to help you along the way. This book and the beginning of my career resemble my transcendence. I didn't just go through this journey for me. I went through it for you. Your ability to help others starts with learning how to help yourself. You don't just act as a model for others to follow; although that is special and important, you also serve as hope for others. I have said from the very beginning that the goal should never be just to obtain a degree and get a job. The goal is to grow as an entire person, to evaluate what makes you who you are, to explore what that means, and to practice building that life in an environment where, if you fail, you can try again.

The best way to find yourself is to lose yourself in the service of others.
—Mahatma Gandhi

Get Lost in the Service of Others

Community service will help you gain experience related to your career. For example, being involved with a volunteer organization can build your leadership skills, and you will find yourself surrounded by selfless people, which is a great environment for you to grow and learn in. You'll also meet people with whom you share similar passions and concerns. By serving others in your community, you can also begin to work on your problem-solving skills, which is something everyone needs in their personal life, and it's something every employer is looking for. During interviews, it is common for potential employers to ask you to name a time when you've overcome a difficult challenge. By being active in community service, you can list times when you've overcome challenges as a team that impacted the greater good of the community, rather than just focusing on your own personal adversities. Employers do also want to hear about how you've overcome personal adversity, but that does not always translate into skills, like teamwork, that are important in the workplace. Furthermore, community service shows an employer that you are willing to go above and beyond the parameters of your job description. They will see that you are driven by something more than just a salary, but a purpose that inspires you. When people see that you have a battle-tested purpose that propels you through adversity, they can trust that, when times get tough within their organization, you will help lead the team through it.

Gratitude

Getting involved in your community is also a great way to flex your gratitude muscle because it encourages a mentality of togetherness and an appreciation for the efforts of others. For example, take a moment to look around you. Consider everything in the room, and all of the manmade structures around you. You did nothing to earn access to all of the technology around you; you were simply born into it and are able to enjoy it today because of the efforts of those who came before you. Try to go through an entire day while internally thanking everyone who has made your life easier and has given you access to something you didn't earn…it will be overwhelming. As you walk on a sidewalk you didn't build, with shoes you didn't make, approaching a building you didn't build, sitting in a chair you didn't invent, so on and so forth, you will find yourself googling the person who invented things you've never thought about. The people who have come before us have solved so many problems, which allows us the ability to focus on the problems of the future, so that we may do the same for the next generation.

Practicing gratitude means becoming more sensitive to all of the things around you that you are grateful for. It means choosing to pass every interaction through the lens of first finding something to be thankful for. In every conversation, as you listen to the person across from you, be thankful for the experiences that have brought them into your life and the wisdom they have gained along the way that they are now sharing with you.

Relationships

As you're learning more about yourself, prioritizing self-awareness, and maximizing your productivity by optimizing your habits, you should also be learning about the various roles you play in your relationships and how you can deliver more value to those around you.

I know this book isn't about relationship advice, but here is some, anyway. First and foremost, it is no one else's responsibility to make you happy. No boyfriend, girlfriend, or partner should be held responsible for making you happy (or vice versa). To build healthy relationships during your college years and throughout the rest of your life, you first need to know yourself well enough to fulfill your own psychological needs, and then find people you can share your happiness with and who will do the same for you. I'm not telling you to abandon your friends who are unhappy or are going through tough times. But, as cliché as it sounds, you can't pour from an empty cup, and if you are constantly bringing an empty cup into your relationships and expecting other people to fill your cup for you, you are eventually going to drain everyone around you.

Being whole attracts whole people. Which is exactly how I ended up marrying a woman who once hated me (and she probably will learn to again) and who was (and still is) way out of my league. When Sarah and I first met, we had a class together. She sat two rows in front of me—when I decided to show up. We never really talked. However, one day, I swiped right on Tinder, and sure enough, we matched. You would probably guess that was how this millennial love story began, but you would be heinously incorrect. We messaged each other and flirted, but the next day, I walked by her on my way to my seat and flirted with the girl behind her instead, like an absolute douche. As if that wasn't enough reason for her to hate my guts, I was the student who would consistently challenge our professor. There were many days when class time would technically be over, but everyone would be too uncomfortable to stand up as I kept the debate alive, peppering the subject matter expert with questions that I believed to be pertinent. So, yeah, I was *that* guy. I was broken, insecure, and crying for attention, and I was never willing to be vulnerable enough to build meaningful relationships. So I pushed people away with my behavior. I went from being that (fill in the blank) to the guy who planned our entire wedding, as a surprise, because I couldn't think of a way to propose that was good enough for milady. We started dating when we met again after my transformation, and I was a completely different person. So many of us often blame others, and we say we haven't met the right person yet, but the truth might be that you've already met the right person, but you weren't the right version of yourself to make it work.

It Takes Courage to Be Vulnerable

As you go through your college years, you'll likely come across situations in your relationships when you will be challenged to speak up for what you know is right. One such occurrence happened soon after I ran into a familiar face on campus. The face had a name, and it was Ray. He and I had gone to middle school and parts of high school together before we parted ways. We played football together as kids, but we weren't close friends; we were associates. Regardless, seeing Ray on campus in those early days of my freshman year felt like taking a huge sigh of relief because it felt like I had someone to show me the ropes, someone I was comfortable with. Throughout that first year, Ray and I became really close.

One morning, Ray, his friend Louis, and I were having breakfast in the campus café. It was a Saturday, and none of us were operating at 100-percent capacity. Ray was talking about this new girl he had been involved with and how they'd just had their first disagreement. He was acting strange about it, he wouldn't really tell us who she was, and he described everything in vague terms. Louis and I could tell that Ray wanted to talk about it but didn't want to open up too much. It felt off. I felt it, and I know Louis felt it, too. During this conversation, Ray uttered words that I let float by at the time, but that now continue to haunt me. He said, "If something happens with her, I swear I will kill myself." That was when Louis and I locked eyes from across the table, almost as if we were saying, "Are you going to say something, or should I?" We both tried talking to him about it more, but as he pushed us away and tried to change the topic of conversation, we let it happen and we moved on. Ray said he didn't mean it, and we believed him. Louis and I talked afterward without Ray, and we both promised we would keep an eye on him. Less than a month later, Ray was found in his dorm room, after he had taken his own life.

I'd sat at a table with him as he had quietly cried out for help, and I did nothing. Those who know me will be shocked to realize that I, of all people, was the person who sat quietly. I have always been the person to speak up, even when it's not my turn (especially when it's not my turn, actually). That is a part of who I am.

You may not like to be the loudest person in the room, but it is essential that you learn to speak up when something is wrong. Don't be afraid to do the unpopular thing. I should have told someone, but I was afraid of how it would make me look, and how it would affect Ray and his ability to trust me. But I'd rather have him here and not trust me than the alternative I have been forced to accept.

One of the most common phrases is "snitches get stitches," and while I know this doesn't quite fall under that category, I fear we have become afraid to speak up because we are more afraid of the repercussions of speaking up than we are of the repercussions that come from our silence. I'm here to tell you that I have many stories and many experiences where I would happily go back and take stitches instead of the tombstones I was given. Find your voice. Stand up for what you think is right, always. Scream what must be heard from the rooftops and do so unapologetically. For every one million people who will tell you to shut up, there may be one who needs to hear what you have to say. Those odds are worth it. Popularity is overrated.

During that same semester when Ray passed, I was faced with another

STEP 5: BUILD CONNECTIONS

challenge when I pledged Alpha Tau Omega. I knew what I was getting myself into because it wasn't a secret that they participated in some hazing, but it was extremely mild. It wasn't anything you'd read about in the newspapers. It was (shamefully) a great time, and I have way more positive memories than negative ones. However, there was one moment in the experience which I will never forget.

It began on the top floor of the library, where we used to have library hours before pledging. We would meet as a pledge class for two to three hours, and we were supposed to use that time to finish our homework before pledging. That was not often the case, but that was the intended purpose. One night, one of my fellow pledges felt they needed to pull an all-nighter to get their work done, so they decided to drink a fruit punch-flavored pre-workout supplement. I thought it was unwise at the time (and still do), but as it turned out, I was glad he did it.

That night, our event was a six-pack race. Like I said, nothing crazy, just an irresponsibly good time. I was excited to start, and I was prepared to win—until I picked up the first can of beer. I realized it was warm—not room-temperature, but like you had just pulled a bowl out of the microwave. Then I cracked the top and realized it was all foam, like it had been shaken or tossed in the dryer. It was at that moment when I realized I'd messed up.

There were enough trash cans for all of us (at least you can say they were prepared). I happened to share my trash can with the idiot (meant as a term of endearment) who'd drank a fruit punch-flavored pre-workout supplement shortly before. As he started puking red, I was immediately alarmed. My initial reaction was to make sure he was alright, but before I could even check on him, one of the brothers cackled, "Look, he's puking red!" All of the brothers in the room proceeded to laugh. None of them knew what we knew—they had no idea why he was puking red, they just thought it was funny. Their failure to acknowledge a clear sign that something could be severely wrong made me question everything.

When I had decided to pledge, I knew that we'd be doing some of this stuff. So I did not feel like I had been lied to or deceived. That was what I—

oddly—had signed up for. I was prepared to have fun, to be the source of entertainment at my own expense. What I was not prepared for was being the most responsible person in a room filled with people who were too stupid to know when a line had been crossed and when to stop before something newsworthy occurred. And yet, in that same room, I was the lowest on the totem pole.

The next day, I spoke with our pledge class and voiced my concerns, explaining that I felt like they had crossed a line and it had to be addressed. Many of the pledges were too afraid to speak out, saying we shouldn't say anything because the hazing would get worse. (See a recurring theme here?) The rest said they didn't mind if I said something, but they weren't willing to go with me. You see, fraternities are often top-down organizations. When you are a pledge, you're nothing. It is like being a soldier at boot camp, only it serves a much less significant purpose. So, it was blasphemous that I would consider questioning the chain of command.

When I went, there was only one brother who bothered to speak to me. I explained to him how I couldn't be a part of a group where I couldn't trust the people within to look out for each other. Sure enough, just a year later, the chapter was on the brink of closing. As I mentioned earlier, the culture that had been in place had caused us to be suspended twice, our chapter was shrinking, and we were not allowed to recruit. In response, the national organization sent a leadership consultant (LC) to check in on us and essentially decide whether they should dissolve the chapter. During my one-on-one with our LC, I told him that if they decided to dissolve the chapter, they should give me one year on my own, as the sole member, to bring the chapter back. He laughed in my face and told me he despised my arrogance, which was ironic since he was supposed to be teaching me how to lead. Fast-forward two years, and I had totally transformed and reimagined our pledge process and our organization. Because I had been brave enough to speak up about the dangerous hazing, I'd opened the door to new, healthier relationships within my fraternity. That was also when I found my calling and realized what I wanted to do with my life: develop leaders through transformational experiences and dismantle toxic cultures in organizations.

Another important lesson in the realm of relationships is understanding the importance of accountability. I once had a friend named Brandon. We both went to the same school at the same time, we both studied engineering, and we both pledged the same fraternity in the same semester. Our stories, when told in parallel, provide some interesting insights. We were going through the same experiences, and we were having many of the same troubles. But here is where our stories begin to diverge. During the second semester of freshman year, we were both taking the same physics course with the same professor. Brandon never turned his homework in on time. My homework was always turned in on time, even though I did not fully understand the content and would get lower grades on those assignments. At the end of the semester, Brandon turned in all his overdue homework—something the professor had made clear at the beginning of the semester was not allowed—and Brandon still received full credit. He passed the course, and I failed it.

Now, you might have read that and thought that Brandon got lucky, or that the situation was unfair. I would argue that people like Brandon are the ones who are getting robbed, not me or anyone else who is truly held accountable for our lack of discipline. Brandon went on to finish engineering school, having similar struggles throughout, and seemingly just getting by. He rode that train all the way through graduation, and even slightly beyond. I can't really tell you whether this is still the case because Brandon and I no longer speak. Here is why:

As you now know, failing college was the best thing to have ever happened to me because it sparked this entire journey and was the beginning of my story that makes it so worth telling. If I hadn't failed, if my professors had passed me along like they had done with Brandon, I might be stuck in a career that I hate and feeling miserable with myself because I don't have the accountability or discipline to build a life that truly fulfills me on a deeper level. I am grateful for everyone who held me accountable. But how did being passed along impact Brandon?

Fast-forward to my graduation, four years after failing my first two semesters and a year after Brandon had graduated, even though we had started school at the same time. Shortly before graduation, I had learned that I'd been accepted into the Teach for America program and would be moving to South Carolina with Sarah (who was my girlfriend at the time and is now my wife). Brandon, being my best friend at the time, was so excited for me and continuously promised that he would help me move. I had countless people saying they were willing to help me move, but there was only one extra seat in the U-Haul truck, and I was counting on Brandon's help. I told everyone, "No, thank you. I only have one extra seat, and it is taken." The day before the big move, I was packing up the truck to make the long trip when I got a call from Brandon. He said he was on his way from work to come help me, but he had not yet eaten, and he had something he wanted to talk to me about. So I said I would take a break from packing the truck since I had not eaten dinner either, and we agreed to meet at a restaurant nearby. I figured it would be good for me to take a break, enjoy a meal with my friend, and talk about whatever was on his mind before we would return to finish packing the truck and get ready for the big moving day.

At the restaurant, we sat down and enjoyed a meal and a few drinks. He began venting about his work situation. It was his first engineering job out of college, and he was struggling. He'd just talked to his supervisor about some time he wanted to request off to come visit me later once I was settled in. His supervisor then made a comment like, "Brandon, you haven't earned the money I've already paid you. What makes you think I am going to approve your time off?"

In hindsight, as a leadership development professional I think this was a terrible way for the supervisor to handle this conversation, but that will be reserved for another book. This was the moment when Brandon realized he had not been performing well at work, and he rightfully became very concerned about his job security. I talked to him more about the situation and offered as much support as I could, and the conversation continued for over two hours. We spent so much time working on his problems on the night before one of the biggest days of my life. As the conversation was coming to an end, he came to the realization that he couldn't help me move—and he left. He didn't even offer to help me finish packing the truck, he just left.

I was stuck. There was no way I was going to call anyone else and ask them to drop everything at the last minute to help me move over six hundred miles away. I had already purchased a one-way flight home from South Carolina for Brandon. I had also purchased a couch and had paid extra to have it express-shipped to the apartment so he would have somewhere to sleep. And, to top it all off, my new apartment was on the third floor, with no elevator, and an outside staircase. Anyone reading this book who is either from the South or has visited the South in August knows how hot and humid it is.

I was now driving alone, with my mom and girlfriend following a few hours behind, and with no one to help me carry the bed my mom would be sleeping on that night, and the couch that would remain empty, up to the third floor. Beyond that, I was fresh out of college and had no money, and I'd just wasted hundreds of dollars to make sure my friend would have somewhere to sleep.

I don't tell this story to demonize Brandon. I don't blame him for the decision he made at the time. I tell this story because I truly believe that being held accountable earlier in my college experience was the catalyst that caused me to change my behaviors, and it made me someone who others could depend on. And I can depend on myself to get things done for my future self and to build the life I want for my future family.

However, the story isn't over. When Brandon called me about a month later, I figured he wanted to talk about what had happened. I expected that he'd apologize and would share the progress he'd been making at work. But that wasn't the case. He called to ask for more help and advice regarding a situation with another friend of his. I was absolutely stunned, too stunned to speak. I let him finish what he had to say, and then I told him:

"I assumed you were calling to ask me how the move went, and to apologize for abandoning me like that. I cannot believe you're calling to ask me for more help, when the last time I helped you, you used me just long enough for it to suit you, and then you left without returning the favor you had promised months before. Don't call me back until you are ready to have a conversation about what you're going to do differently to make sure I can actually depend on you in the future. By the way, before we hang up, did you do any work that weekend? Did you do anything that could have helped you improve your situation at work?" (I had made sure to have Wi-Fi installed at my new apartment before our arrival so that he could work remotely, if needed.)

Do you know what he said?

"No. I didn't do anything work-related that weekend."

That was the end of our conversation—and our friendship.

Do you know what else I learned from my friendship with Brandon? In life, as you begin to accomplish bigger and bigger things, you will encounter people you love who will want to join you, who want to be there with you; but the truth is, sometimes, their own lack of accountability will prevent them from joining you in that place to celebrate that success with you. When that moment comes, it will be time for you to leave them in the previous chapter of your life. Some people enter your life for a reason, others enter it for a season. Appreciate them for the role they've played, and be grateful for the time you've had together, but see it as a sign that it is time to move on. You are going to have similar experiences with some of your hometown or high school friends when you go away to college, and the same process is going to occur again when you graduate. I share this with you because it is really important to understand which characters in your life story should make it to your next chapter because they will help you write it. If those characters aren't developing throughout your story line, they need to be left in an earlier chapter.

This also applies to weeding out toxic people from your life. When I first moved in with my grandma during college, I had a best friend named William who I pretty much spent every day with. He had a naturally infectious attitude; he would walk into a room and introduce himself to every single soul there. The kid just oozed charisma. But he didn't do it for attention, he did it because he genuinely wanted to know every single person in the room. He would see someone months later, someone he had only met once at a party, and he'd remember every single thing about them. He was the definition of someone whom everyone knew. As admirable a character as William was, socializing was his primary focus. He had every ounce of potential to be something special, but he couldn't bring himself to align his priorities with what would ultimately lead him down a path to a fulfilling life. Sound familiar? That was probably why we were so close at the time.

When I moved into my grandma's house, William and I began to grow apart as my responsibilities started taking me in a different direction and William started to show a different side of himself. For example, when I would have to leave parties early because my grandma wasn't feeling well or because I had to take care of my puppy, Luna, William grew frustrated. You see, once I became inconvenient to him, I became irrelevant.

What I learned from this experience was that my responsibilities almost became repellent to irresponsible people like William. The people I was better off without naturally faded from my life. Over time, the kind of people I ultimately wanted to surround myself with were the people who stayed in my life. These were the people who wanted to see me succeed, even when it was inconvenient for them. They were the ones who had their shit together enough to be able to step in and help me when I needed them, because they knew I would do the same in return.

As much as I have preached throughout this book about the importance of building self-awareness and growth, your relationships are the most important things in your life. In his book *Outliers*, Malcolm Gladwell shares how the depth of relationships within communities leads to healthier outcomes for everyone. Research on lottery winners shows that they are no happier with their lives than the average person. Why? Because most lottery winners quit their jobs, a place that gave them meaning and purpose while also creating a friend group of sorts, then they sell their houses to move into nicer places (typically in new communities where they don't know anyone), and they find people in their families and friend groups asking for money. Suddenly, they feel like their relationships are no longer authentic, and everyone who once loved them for who they are now just want something from them. You hear the same stories from professional athletes after they get drafted.

The truth is the relationships portion of this book is the most important one. College also creates an opportunity to expose you to a diverse group of people from places and backgrounds you may have never been exposed to. What happens outside of the classroom is more important than what happens inside the classroom. No one has asked me what my GPA was since I graduated. If I had chosen to have a GPA that was 0.2 points higher than some of the friends I have now, my life would be much worse. Surrounding yourself with people who enhance your life in a multitude of ways, while also learning how to love them and yourself properly, is much more likely to lead to a life of success and happiness than any college degree.

Sharing Your Goals

As you continue to build connections and develop valuable, healthy relationships, you'll also have the opportunity to form deeper bonds through shared goals. Ryan Cass is the founder of Won Day, and he coaches college students and young professionals through the goal-setting process to establish a foundation for sustained success. When I interviewed him for my podcast, he shared insights from various research studies. According to the Association for Talent Development, those who wrote down their goals were 40 percent more likely to achieve them, and those who shared their goals with others were 60–70 percent more likely to achieve those goals.

These insights highlight the importance of building the right community around you. Not only should you practice writing down your goals and building systems to help you achieve them, but you should also build a friend group where you can all share your goals and hold each other accountable to them.

By sharing your goals, you can achieve a few things. First, you have an accountability system. When those friends see you, they can ask about your progress. On the flip side, when they see you exhibiting behaviors that might be contradicting your goals, they can hold you in check. Second, any of your friends who are farther along in a particular aspect of their life that you are trying to work on can help you in that area. For example, Ryan is an avid runner.

In fact, he qualified for the Boston Marathon. I, on the other hand, am not a seasoned runner. Running was never my thing. I was a lineman on the high school football team, if that puts anything into perspective for you. I got into powerlifting for a while after high school, until I let my fitness and health fall off the wagon…hard. Then, a few years after college, after I had continued to gain weight and get into worse and worse shape, I decided to start running. I liked the idea of running because it is something you can do at any hour, like having a gym that never closes, and it is free (minus the cost of shoes). But I had no idea where to start. Having a friend like Ryan was extremely helpful because I knew I could talk to him about my struggles. He has been there and done that, so he could help me achieve my goals in running and fitness.

By sharing your goals, you can also find people who are in the same spot as you, someone you can talk to about the experience, someone you can share your frustrations with, someone who can empathize with you in a unique way.

And finally, by sharing your goals, you can be an inspiration to others in your network. They might read your goals and think, *Wow, I can't believe he/she/they are doing all of that…I want to get in on the action.* In this way, you can act as a mentor to someone else, which will give you a sense of a higher purpose. Now you aren't just achieving your goals for yourself, you are also doing it for those around you, those who care about you and look up to you. There is nothing more empowering.

If you have a friend you can't share your goals with, they are not your friend. Protect your goals. Share them like they are sacred. If someone in your circle talks down on your goals, they don't belong in that inner circle. They are no longer a friend; they can be an acquaintance you say hello to and enjoy drinks with on occasion, but they don't deserve access to your dreams.

This brings us to the rule of thirty-three, which states that you should spend 33 percent of your time with people who mentor you, 33 percent of your time with people who are your peers, and 33 percent of your time mentoring others. That is the ultimate balance for learning and development. If you spend too much time with mentors, they will share information at a rate faster than you can absorb and try out. If you spend too much time with your peers, you won't have enough new information to share with your counterparts and test the validity of it with them. On the other hand, your peers will feel comfortable pushing back on and asking questions that you maybe failed to consider when you were with your mentor. They will also allow you to test theories at scale. For example, if I have ten friends who are all in the same place as me and who have the same problem, we can all test a solution a mentor provided to see what the success rate looks like. Did it only work for one of us? Why? Then, once we learn new information, we can test it with a group of our peers and find how to leverage it to generate results. We should then be able to teach it to others we mentor. The best way to know how well you understand something is not to teach it to your peers, but to teach it to someone who may not understand it as much as you do, someone you mentor. They will certainly ask questions you would have never considered. And the best way to test how well you know something is to see how well you can explain it in the simplest terms possible. If you can't explain it simply, you don't understand it well enough. This is where you learn to deliver value with the knowledge you have.

The interesting thing about the rule of thirty-three is that one person can play all three roles in your life. The same person who is your mentor in fitness can also be your mentee in business and your peer in another aspect of life. The important thing is to find balance between those three roles in your life. I discovered at the end of my college experience that some of my closest friends became people I was mentoring more than 90 percent of the time. We were growing in different directions and at different paces, and it became clear to me that the things I valued were not important enough to them. I decided to audit my time, and I realized that I was spending too much time with people who were throwing off this balance and were not delivering enough value for me and my personal development. The relationships weren't mutually beneficial. I decided to distance myself from those people, and I found that my life became more rewarding. It was uncomfortable at times because I had relied on those people for validation. But once I removed myself from the validation they once offered me, I was better able to identify opportunities to grow. I became less focused on the value I had to share and more focused on where I needed to obtain more value so I could share it in the future. I also learned throughout that process that there were things I had told those people that weren't true. I was overstepping my knowledge and sharing wisdom I didn't have. This was why it was important to find the right balance.

Here is how you can implement the rule of thirty-three in your life. Start by writing a general outline of your schedule. What does your average week look like? Who do you spend time with, and about how much time do you spend with them? Next to the names of those people, write an estimated percentage of how much time you spend in each role while you're with them. You will probably discover that you spend an abundance of time with peers. I do this workshop with students and young professionals alike, and on average, they say they spend 70 percent of their time with their peers, 20–25 percent of their time with mentors, and the remaining time with mentees. This is when it is important to have discussions with your friends and peers. Find out who has knowledge to share in certain aspects of life, and then challenge them to take on more of a mentor role in the group.

Watch how much your friend group grows together when each member is challenged to lead in their respective areas of strength. They become more confident, and everyone grows together.

Conclusion

College is a fertile environment for transformation. You are removed from your original tribe, with an opportunity to build a new one. This allows you to call into question everything you have ever been taught about life. Take advantage of this by treating yourself like a psychology experiment, exposing yourself to new people and new possibilities, and do so with the intention to define what happiness, success, and significance looks like for you. Write down the things you value most in this world, and draw a feedback loop for each of them. Map out the process of building success in each of those aspects of your life, and never compromise on them.

Finally, remember this: Your greatness is not your own. It does not belong to you; it is something you cultivate to share with others. You don't start a farm to eat all your crops. We all enjoy the comfort provided by the shade of trees we did not plant, water, or grow. Our job in this life is to plant, water, and grow those trees for others. May this book guide you on the beginning chapter of that journey. I realized I could never do enough to thank everyone in my life for all they have done for me. This is because I have been given a forest larger than one I would ever have been able to grow on my own, and for that I am eternally grateful. I will never be able to return the favor. So, instead, I have chosen to devote my life to empowering others to plant trees, in the hope that, one day, others can be as blessed as I have been. Thank you for being one of those blessings.

Thank you, from the bottom of my heart, for the opportunity to share my story and the wisdom I have gained along the way.

If you have found the lessons in this book to be valuable, please leave a review on Amazon to make sure other people who need to read this book will see it. Be sure to not only give it a rating but to also write some details about why you gave it that rating.

If you want to hear more content from me about how I turned my transformational college experience into a successful career and a life of happiness and fulfillment, subscribe to my podcast, *The Pursuit of Self-Actualization*. In addition to sharing the rest of my story as it unfolds, I also interview successful athletes, authors, entrepreneurs, speakers, and world-renowned researchers as I continue to explore what it means to become the best version of yourself.

I also do my best to be very accessible on social media. I am lucky to have a unique name, so search Dante DiBattista or @dantedibattista on any platform and you will be able to find me.

If you are ever looking for a speaker to come to your school or business, you can inquire on my website at https://dantedibattista.com/.

Acknowledgments

As you can imagine, there is a long list of people who have helped me along the way. If your name is on this list, just know that I have dedicated my entire life to becoming the best person I can possibly be because I owe it to you. I carry myself as a representation of you, and because of that, I will forever strive to succeed more in order to make your investment in my development worth it. Thank you, from the bottom of my heart, and with my utmost love and respect.

Mrs. Karen Daly,

This woman was the first person at Widener University to believe in me. I wouldn't have made it past freshman year without her as my adviser. Her advocacy for me as a person is one of the few reasons I decided to continue with school. She was my mother at school when I needed it. She is the one who taught me how to utilize a planner and my syllabi to outline my semester, but she also taught me how to believe in myself by following her example.

Dr. Luke Ayers,

After I decided to major in psychology, I was assigned Dr. Ayers as my adviser. He had extremely big shoes to fill because of the immense impact Mrs. Daly had had on me, and he didn't hesitate to rise to the occasion. When I stepped into his office and talked to him about my past and my goals, he encouraged me to pursue them, regardless of what my transcript said. He set clear expectations for what I needed to do, and he told me that it would not be easy but that I could do it. He was honest with me from day one, and he advocated for me when there weren't many reasons (on paper) to do so.

Dr. Arthur Schwartz,

The day we crossed paths changed my life forever. Dr. Schwartz and the leadership development programs he designed created an environment that allowed me to thrive and grow into the leader I am today. Without him, I would not be where I am in my career and in my life. He embodies integrity, thoughtfulness, and humility in a way that I have yet to see replicated by anyone else. When I travel and speak, I share our story. How we met, how it changed my life forever, and how I've devoted my life to being the Arthur in someone else's story. Thank you for the example you've set for me. I hope I've made you proud.

Mom,

I had to save the best for last. My mother spent countless hours on the phone with my teachers and principals, as a result of my behavior in school. She always stuck up for me and believed in me. I was once invited to talk on a podcast called *Success in SC*, where entrepreneurs and thought leaders from all over the state of South Carolina are invited to share how their work is molding the future of the state, all in an effort to highlight the incredible talent we have to offer. During that episode, I was asked about my key to success in life. My response was an unwavering belief in myself. I don't care what the odds are, I don't care what obstacles are in my way. I will always believe in myself. I'd rather bet on myself and lose than bet against myself and win. That mindset comes from my mom. She's always pushed me to chase my dreams, even when I didn't know what they were. She trusted that I would learn my lessons and grow up…eventually. My love, respect, and gratitude are unconditional for all these individuals, especially this angel.

If I can offer one last piece of advice, it would be this: give people their roses while they are still here. Don't wait until they're gone to tell their story. I wrote this book to act as an eternal rose garden for the people who have made my life worth living, and for those whom I choose to live on for who have left before my story is finished.

References

Costandi, Moheb. 2016. *Neuroplasticity.* Cambridge: The MIT Press.

Daum, Kevin. 2012. "How to Make Great Decisions (Most of the Time)." *Inc.,* October 16. https://www.inc.com/kevin-daum/how-to-make-great-decisions-most-of-the-time.html.

Downes, Stephen M., and Zalta, Edward N., ed. 2021. "Evolutionary Psychology." *The Stanford Encyclopedia of Philosophy (Spring 2021 Edition).* https://plato.stanford.edu/archives/spr2021/entries/evolutionary-psychology/.

Duneier, Stephen. "How to Achieve Your Most Ambitious Goals." TEDx video. https://www.youtube.com/watch?v=TQMbvJNRpLE.

Havekes, Robbert. "Sleep Deprivation and Memory Problems." TEDx video. https://www.youtube.com/watch?v=F39IBJZlsek.

McGonigal, Kelly. "How to Make Stress Your Friend." TED video, 2013. https://www.ted.com/talks/kelly_mcgonigal_how_to_make_stress_your_friend/transcript?language=en.

Mcleod, Saul, PhD. 2022. "Maslow's Hierarchy of Needs." *Simply Psychology* (blog), April 4. https://www.simplypsychology.org/maslow.html.

Meyer, Jerrold S., and Quenzer, Linda F. 2004. *Psychopharmacology: Drugs, the Brain, and Behavior.* Oxford University Press.

Ravilochan, Teju. 2021. "The Blackfoot Wisdom that Inspired Maslow's Hierarchy." *Resilience,* June 18. https://www.resilience.org/stories/2021-06-18/the-blackfoot-wisdom-that-inspired-maslows-hierarchy/.

Roberts, Nicole F. 2020. "Emotional and Physical Pain Are Almost the Same—to Your Brain." *Forbes,* February 14. https://www.forbes.com/sites/nicolefisher/2020/02/14/emotional--physical-pain-are-almost-the-sameto-your-brain/?sh=197aa98046c1.

Sullivan, Dan, and Hardy, Benjamin P. 2020. *Who Not How.* Hay House Business.

About the Author

Dante's story expands far beyond the college experience. Dante now serves as a leadership development coach, consultant, and public speaker for organizations around the world. Executives from Fortune 500 companies seek guidance on how to handle their most challenging people problems across the organization and create environments where employees can bring their best, whole selves to work. He has helped companies transform from toxic work cultures to award-winning "Best Places to Work," according to Best Companies Group. He also serves as a facilitator at some of the top MBA and leadership development programs in the country, including the MIT Leadership Center.

If you are looking for a motivational and inspirational speaker, a leadership development trainer and facilitator, or a mentor, do not hesitate to reach out to info@dantedibattista.com to learn more about the suite of services available.